Thérèse Larkin

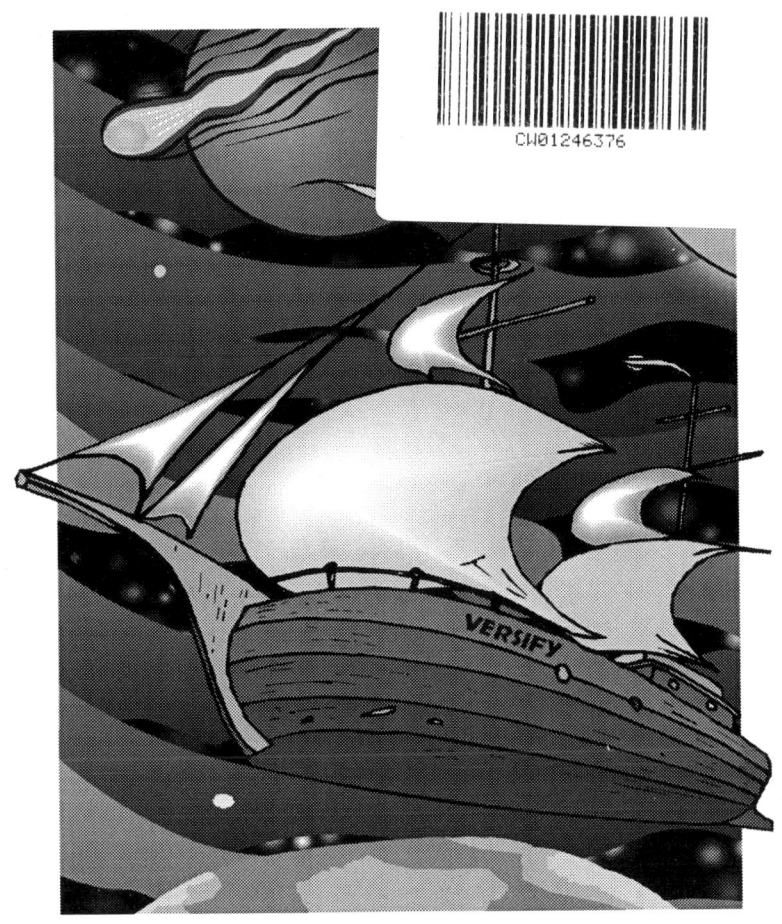

POETIC VOYAGES SCOTLAND

Edited by Helen Chatwin

First published in Great Britain in 2001 by
YOUNG WRITERS
Remus House,
Coltsfoot Drive,
Peterborough, PE2 9JX
Telephone (01733) 890066

All Rights Reserved

Copyright Contributors 2001

HB ISBN 0 75433 220 9
SB ISBN 0 75433 221 7

FOREWORD

Young Writers was established in 1991 with the aim to promote creative writing in children, to make reading and writing poetry fun.

This year once again, proved to be a tremendous success with over 88,000 entries received nationwide.

The Poetic Voyages competition has shown us the high standard of work and effort that children are capable of today. It is a reflection of the teaching skills in schools, the enthusiasm and creativity they have injected into their pupils shines clearly within this anthology.

The task of selecting poems was therefore a difficult one but nevertheless, an enjoyable experience. We hope you are as pleased with the final selection in *Poetic Voyages Scotland* as we are.

CONTENTS

James Aiton Primary School
    Fraser Wilson   1
    David Young   1
    Christina Bristow   2
    Jade Telfer   2
    Sally Hackett   3
    Emma Fisher   3

Alexandra Parade Primary School
    Stacy Stott   4
    Mark McAllister & Michael Tidser   4
    Allan Casey   5
    Gary Leggat   5
    Sean O'Neill   6
    Robert Payne   6
    Linsay McPhail   7
    Daryl Cameron   7
    Garry Bower   8
    Rebecca Traynor   8

Arden Primary School
    Andrew Mundt   9
    Gary Rodger   9
    Danielle Mathieson   10
    Caroline Gentle   10
    Stuart Sherlock   11
    Stephanie Sawers   11
    Scott MacDonald   11

Atholl Preparatory School
    Emma Gallacher   12
    Shuto Fukuyo   12
    Rosalind Philips   12
    Jennifer Sinclair   13
    Amy Douglas   13

      Lara Davidson   14

Bargeddie Primary School
    Kimberley Grierson   14
    Kelsey Brown   15
    Scott Cullen   15
    Robyn Jenkins   16
    Amie McLaughlin   16
    Stephanie Campbell   17
    Kirsten Savage   17
    Donna Wilkinson   18
    Ross Bell   18
    Robert Totten   19
    Gemma Cochrane   19

Burnbrae Primary School
    David Murray   20
    Ashley Peacock   20
    Nicole Harris   21
    Amanda Littlejohn   21
    James Johnston   22
    Christopher Black   22
    Nicola Murray   23
    John Buchanan   24
    Christopher Dunne   24
    Jade Reid   25
    Jade Macleod   26
    Marie Dempster   27
    Pamela Howson   28

Clober Primary School
    James Eilliott   29
    Maegan Shearer   29
    Katie Gourlay   30
    Chris Stevenson   30
    Thomas Matthew   31
    Katie Telfer   32
    Kirsty Gray   32

Ross Taylor	33
Douglas Bouttell	33
Fiona Bain	34
Gemma Powell	35
Karen Ferguson	36
Mhairi Millar	36
Johnathan McNabb	37
Scott Roger	38
James Crane	38
Ross Byford	39
Mark Welsh	39
Kyle Buchanan	40
Craig Williamson	40
Robbie Grey	41
Craig Purdie	41
Scott Watson	42
Ross Easton	42
Fiona Dickson	43
Mark Saunders	43
Scott Maxwell	44
Amy Louise Hendry	44
Mark Bohonek	45
Greig Roger	45
Nicola Raworth	46
Calum Shaw	47
Richard Pollock	48
Jason McCabe	49
Gary Hutchison	50
Daryl Bell	51

Corpus Christi Primary School

Miriam McKay	51
Jennifer Scott	52
Catherine MacMillan	53
Jane Harrison	54
Anthony Hughes	54
Caroline Maxwell	55

Drumry Primary School
    Amanda Fraser   55
    Kevin Clark   55
    Ashleigh Wilson   56
    Barrie Davidson   57
    Thomas Curran   57
    Stephanie Siller   58
    Wendy Sharpe   58
    Karina Duncanson   59
    Jamielee Downie   59
    Ashleigh Hinson   60
    Jamie Sweeney   61

Eastfield Primary School
    Craig Edwardson   62
    Craig McDonald   63
    Chloe Hunter   63
    Sarah Falconer   64
    Ross Johnston   64
    Megan Greene   65
    Louise Warden   65
    Ryan Maginess   66
    Nikki Andrew   66
    Fiona Dalrymple   67
    Stuart Kearney   67
    Martina Salveta   68
    Douglas Morton   68
    Alan Stewart   69
    Ross Cook   69
    Natalie Fleming   70
    Neil Buncow   70
    Amy Pollock   71
    David Colquhoun   71
    Keith Sinclair   72

Garthamlock Primary School
    Mark Rodgers   72
    Ashleigh Mitchell   72

Patricia McGonagle	73
James MacLeod	73
Christopher Murphy	73
Alexander Campbell	74
Jordan McGlinchey	74
Ashley Andrews	74

Holmlea Primary School

Barry Milligan	75
Isla Dundas	75
Lynsey Ferguson	76
Anna Papadaki	76
Jamie Cameron	77
Craig Miller	77
Angus Kean	78
Danny Leinster	78
Raisah Din	79
Heather Archibald	80
Zubair Aslam	80
Emma Andrew	81
Darren Ashton	81
Emma Lee	82
Fiona Young	82
Saimah Din	83
Scott Fulton	83
Graeme Smart	84
Emma Strickland	84
Lee McColl	85
Lee Clark	86
Rebecca Pearson	86
Emma Malcolm	87

Kildrum Primary School

George Spence	87
Karina McLeod	88
Graham Whitton	89
Spike Campbell	89
Laura Grant	90

Andrew Fyffe	90
Marcus Angiolini	91
Misha Connell	91
Scott Tominey	92
Claire Laura Semple	92
David Easton	93
Lisa Devine	93
Marina Elizabeth Hunter Phillips	94
Sheona Cullen	94
Aileen Alicia Wyatt	95
Matthew Love	95
Emma Sadler	96
James William Dewar	96
Danielle Gilmour	97
Jamie Pearson	97
Dionne Tominey	97
Euan Russell	98
Caroline Blair Wheeler Williams	98

Mosspark Primary School

Barry Douglas	98
Catherine Collins	99
Fraser McIntyre	99
Craig MacDonald	100
Shafaq Khan	100
Ashley Prior	101
Holly McDonald	102
Diane Dick	102
Amanda Gow	103
Ross MacDonald	104
Laura-Marie Gormley	104
Amy Pollok	105
Iain Slorance	106
Jacqueline Lindsay	107
Christopher McCabe	108
Gemma Coulston	109
John Hugh Connor	110
Jade Stewart	111

Nicola Munro	112
Mairi Campbell	113
Marc MacCallum	114
Jennifer Hutton	115
Greg Quinn	116
Paul Milne	117
Claire Dyer	117
Sara MacCallum	118
Grant McKigen	118
Keira McLellan	119
Amy McLellan	119
Steven Barrowman	120
Ross Carstairs	120
Chirelle Fitzpatrick	121
Stephanie Gormley	122
Robert Orr	122
Hayley Weinman	123
Michaela Muir	123
Kirsty Aitcheson	124
Ross Hocknull	124
Angela McManus	125
Omar Azam	125
Hayley Smith	126
Alan McGarrity	126

Notre Dame Primary School

Lewa Thomas	127
Nabila Arshad	127
Claire Reilly	128
Sarah Graham	128
Laura May Frize	129
Colm McGuire	130
Victoria Culshaw	130
Kirsty Douglas	131
Stuart Armit	131

Ravenswood Primary School
    Rebecca Fergus   132
    Paul Coulter   132
    Andrew Carmichael   132
    Rebecca Main   133
    Cairn MacFarlane   133
    Ross McLachlan   134
    Joanna Cameron   134
    Holly Scotland   134
    Lynn Baillie   135
    Daryn Murphy   135
    Alister Yule   136
    Sarah Brynes   137
    Meltem Kesal   137

Rogerfield Primary School
    Katrina Woods   138
    Sarah Baillie   138
    Scott Wilson   138
    Ashleigh Gillies   139
    Jade Grimason   139
    Steven Baillie   139
    Ashley Loughran   140
    Karen McFarlane   140
    Kayleigh Baldwin   141

St Angela's Primary School, Glasgow
    Stephen McCann   141
    Halim Boussouara   142
    Liam O'Reilly   142
    Sabrena Iqbal   143
    Claire Turner   143
    Mishka Krause   144
    John Murphy   144
    Anthony Healy   145
    Nicky Starnes   146
    Deborah Layden   146
    Jamie Clark   147

James McArdle	148
Gina Ventre	149
Sean Bill	150
Robert Wynn	150
Danielle McCabe	151
Kenny Chu	151
Lucy Jackson	152
Lindsey Boyle	152
Kimberley Hendry	153
Lyndsay MacSween	154
Tariq Boussouara	154
Ryan Hooper	155
Rachael Docherty	155
Aislinn Dowling	156

St Bartholomew's Primary School, Glasgow

Erin Tierney	156
Nicola Mulheron	157
Josh Henderson	158

St Cadoc's Primary School, Glasgow

Natalie Casci	158
Katrina Evans	159
Patrick Hamill	159
Suzanne Oswald	160
Siobhan Cameron	160
Sarah Wallace	161
Amy Ford	162
Jennifer Lynn	162
Sean Pickering	163
Amy Rowe	163
Fiona Pittman	164
Emma Anderson	164

St Hilary's Primary School, Glasgow

Joanne McKenna	165
Katie Thomson	165
Elaine Veitch	166

Emma Fulton	166
Michael Cusack	167
Katy Gallagher	167
Gordon Quinn	168
Daniel Law	168
Julie Marie Blake	169
David McGeever	169
Michael Linskey	170
James Fowlie	170
Gemma Connolly	171
Kevin O'Boyle	171
Mhairi Stringer	172
Caroline Anne McHugh	172
Katie Baptie	172
James Scanlan	173
Richard Lynn	173
Emma Fletcher	174
Stephen Dickson	174
Christopher John Barbara	174
Daniel McAinsh	175
Stephen Dingwall	175
Claire Neil	176
Stefanie Kennedy	176
Greg Lemon	177
Daniel Guy	177
Christina Lila Midgley	178

St Jerome's Primary School, Glasgow

Ashleigh Buchan	178
Sean McGhee	179
Peter McGowan	179
Kevin Callaghan	180
Daryl Knox	180
Colette Mackenzie	181
Sean Ferguson	181
Kim Marie Bradley	182
Jonathan Ralston	182

St Louise's Primary School, Glasgow
- Kieran Devlin — 183
- Greg Galbraith — 183
- Stacey Anne Quinn — 184
- Kieran Rooney — 184
- Nicola Claffey — 185
- Lisa McCarron — 185
- Nicole Bradley — 185
- Samantha Weldon — 186
- Lyndsay Swan — 186
- Cheryl Louise Hume — 187
- Laura McGarrell — 188

St Machan's Primary School, Glasgow
- Michael Quigley — 188
- Roisin Convery — 188
- Daryl Robertson — 189
- Kirsten Hardie — 189

St Peter's Primary School, Glasgow
- Claire Neilan — 190
- Stephanie Man — 190
- Laura McSheffrey — 191
- Sinead McLaughlin — 191
- Anthony Cosimini — 192
- Mark Tully — 192
- David Smith — 193
- Nicolle Campbell — 193
- David Whitehill — 193
- Rachel Johnstone — 194
- Ross Boyle — 194
- Kashif Din — 195
- Sam Tulleth — 195
- Kerri Whitelaw — 196

Tinto Primary School
- Rachael Aitken — 196

West Coats Primary School
    Danielle Sharkey   197
    Alice Watson   197
    Deborah Wilson   198
    Joanne Lang   198
    Jamie McPherson   198
    Alison Louise Wright   199
    Louise Thomson   199
    Lori Allen   200

Westfield Primary School
    Kevin Grant   200
    Carrie McFadyen   201
    Emma Kirkland   201
    Duncan Howie   202
    Clair Wilson   203
    Diane Baker   204
    Stephanie Milliken   204
    Lewis Johnstone   205
    Elissa Moffat   206
    Alan Bickerton   207

Whitelees Primary School
    Yvonne Carchrie   207
    Robyn Wade   208
    Emma Davie   209
    David Bain   210

The Poems

SUPER-DUPER MIXTURE!

Smoke so high,
Right into the sky,
Fiery fearsome smell,
Oh only if I could tell,
A spicy staggering fierce and frenzy smell,
Oh Grandma dear, well, well, well,
Grandma if I could tell you oh how you would rise,
For Grandma dear, you're in for a big surprise.

Fraser Wilson (9)
James Aiton Primary School

COLOURS FROM THE DEPTHS

Frothing, fearsome, fiery too,
Brilliant, bubbling, bright and blue,
Gurgling, graceful, grim and green,
Not any hesitation to be seen.
From the depths smells arise,
From a rat, four horses' eyes,
O Grandma, you I sure will miss,
Once you get a whiff of this.

David Young (9)
James Aiton Primary School

THE FINDING OF THE FOX

As the winds blew soft in the afternoon,
There she was the black fox,
Gracefully she skimmed over the grass,
Gently her paws trod like she was not even there,
And then *pounce!*
She caught her prey, a little, little mouse,
And as I sat under the tree,
The wind changed,
She got my scent,
Left like she had not been there
Had it just been a dream?

Christina Bristow
James Aiton Primary School

A CHRISTMAS WISH

I wish . . .
All sickness to be cured
All children to be shown love
For help for the homeless
For respect for old people
There was no famine in the world
There was peace in the world.

Jade Telfer (11)
James Aiton Primary School

ONE LOVELY DAY

One lovely day when the owls were asleep,
The birds were singing, tweet, tweet, tweet.
The grasshoppers were jumping high,
The butterflies were fluttering into the sky.
The sun was shining on the grass,
Tom was waiting for the fox to pass.
Then there he saw it like a flash of light,
The pond started rippling and then turned bright.
It crouched slowly then pounced for its prey,
It took the mouse and carried it away.

Sally Hackett (9)
James Aiton Primary School

THE BLACK FOX

Tom is always on his own,
He really wants to be at home.
He's sitting in the green grass,
Waiting for the fox to pass.
The fox came to hunt for mice,
Foxes are graceful, they are really nice.
The fox trotted back into the woods,
To feed his family with the delicious food.
Tom was excited he wanted to keep it,
He wondered if he should tell anyone
                        or keep it a secret.

Emma Fisher (10)
James Aiton Primary School

WHITE HORSES

The raging sea is a herd of rough stallions.
Their wild heads crash, plash and leap as they bolt, buck
                and gallop towards the muddy beach.
The sandy shore and crumbling cliff wait for their deafening
                      and powerful charge.
The choppy horses, puffing, are raging and dramatic.
The rain pelts.
The wind howls.
The lightning flickers.
The thunder rumbles.
The gale-like wild stallions are ravenous.
The silky tornado crashes.

Stacy Stott (11)
Alexandra Parade Primary School

PETS

What pet have you got?
A snake, a cat or a dog?
Is it big? Is it small?
Does it walk, or does it crawl?
Has it fur, skin or scales?
How many legs or how many tails?
Is your pet young or old?
Does it do whatever it's told?
Do you think you look like your pet?
It has got your features
That's a bet!

Mark McAllister & Michael Tidser (11)
Alexandra Parade Primary School

WHITE HORSES

The raging sea is a herd of rough stallions.
Their choppy heads leap, crash and foam as they
      gallop, prance and leap towards the golden beach.
The lonely shore and craggy cliff wait for their dramatic
                        and powerful charge.
The glassy horses, snorting and puffing, are raging and furious.
The rain lashes.
The wind blasts.
The lightning flickers.
The thunder roars.
The windy, alert stallions are famished.
The smooth wild waves roll.

Allan Casey (11)
Alexandra Parade Primary School

WHITE HORSES

The rough sea is a herd of unruly stallions.
Their billowing heads break the choppy sea and crash as they
leap and canter towards the deserted beach.
The golden shore and craggy cliff wait for their deafening
and frightening charge.
The grey horses, snorting and puffing, are devastating
and destructive.
Rain lashes down.
Wind blasts.
Lightning flashes.
Thunder rumbles.
The violent, rough stallions are starving.
The shining, blistering sea booms.

Gary Leggat (11)
Alexandra Parade Primary School

WHITE HORSES

The raging sea is a herd of rowdy stallions.
Their choppy heads leap, churn and splash as they gallop towards the deserted beach.
The muddy shore and craggy cliffs wait for their hurricane and dramatic charge.
The billowing horses, neighing and whinnying, are destructive and deafening.
The rain lashes.
The wind wails.
The lightning flares.
The thunder echoes.
The stormy, brave stallions are famished.
The dull, violent sky crashes.

Sean O'Neill (11)
Alexandra Parade Primary School

WHITE HORSES

The aquamarine sea is a herd of uncontrollable stallions.
Their raging heads are crashing, racing and swirling as they canter, leap and gallop towards the deserted beach.
The golden shore and bare cliff wait for their devastating and destructive charge.
The rough horses, blowing and puffing, are furious and powerful.
The rain buckets down.
The wind howls.
The lighting flashes.
The thunder booms.
The windy, alert stallions are starving.
The silky, gusting wind echoes.

Robert Payne (11)
Alexandra Parade Primary School

WHITE HORSES

The choppy sea is a herd of unruly stallions.
Their grey heads crash, pound and thunder
as they jump, kick and gallop towards the sandy beach.
The golden shore and jagged cliff wait for their furious storm
and deafening charge.
The heaving horses, puffing and blowing, are devastating
and destructive.
The rain lashes.
The wind blows.
The lightning flares.
The thunder echoes.
The violent, alert stallions are ravenous.

Linsay McPhail (11)
Alexandra Parade Primary School

THE STORMY SEA

The worried men in their rowing boat
heaving like the wind to get back to shore.

The slimy seaweed binding the fish like
a snake wrapped around someone's neck.

The angry waves roaring like a lion
with a thorn stuck in its foot.

The driftwood snapping like a crocodile
snapping its teeth to get a man.

The thunder and lightning striking the sea creatures
back into their homes under the sea.

Daryl Cameron (11)
Alexandra Parade Primary School

WHITE HORSES

The wild sea is a herd of uncontrollable stallions.
Their heaving heads surge, swirl and swish as they gallop,
jump and leap towards the isolated beach.
The exposed shore and jaggy cliff wait for their destructive
and powerful charge.
The wild horses, snorting and puffing, are frightening
and raging.
The rain teems.
The wind batters.
The lightning flashes.
The thunder booms.
The gale-like courageous stallions are ravenous.
The shiny, blustery sea crashes.
The beach is about to be taken.

Garry Bower (11)
Alexandra Parade Primary School

TEACHERS

Some teachers are crazy, they walk with a swagger.
I wonder, oh wonder, what's in their carrier bag?
They sit at their desks, and just ask, ask, ask!
'Now what's for today?' the teacher will say
'Look at the board and don't dare look away.
The head teacher is on her way.'
None of us would take the mick, but we wonder
who's going to be the teacher's pick.
Some act real cool with all their class rules.

Rebecca Traynor (11)
Alexandra Parade Primary School

THE THING

It's hiding in the closet
Underneath the stairs
It ate my toys, my school stuff too
Even my cuddly bears

It's hiding in the closet
Round and green and mean
Big and ugly and hairy
I think you'd better be wary

It's hiding in the closet
It ate my very last shoe
Listen, I hear something
There it is
Boo.

Andrew Mundt (9)
Arden Primary School

KITTENS

Baby cats are called kittens,
They don't wear mittens,
Instead they have paws,
With very sharp claws.
They're not that tall,
They shiver and fall,
They can't run far,
That's what baby cats are.

Gary Rodger (9)
Arden Primary School

THE STARS

The stars are bright
As bright as the moonlight
That shines so bright
The stars are as bright as
The sunshine's light
In the blue sky they shine
So bright
They twinkle like a diamond
Twinkle so bright
Shine so light
Everyone loves them in the dark nights.

Danielle Mathieson (9)
Arden Primary School

STARS

Stars are bright
Bright and light
They're shiny blue.
They come at night-time
Just when it is your bedtime.
Sparkling in your room
Like a bright air balloon.
They help you see at night
When you're afraid of the dark.

Caroline Gentle (9)
Arden Primary School

MY VOYAGE

We were on a voyage,
It was to the moon but
we didn't know where we were.
I thought that I was at Saturn and
they thought that they were at the moon.
Then we looked at the laptops and
they said it was only a play.

Stuart Sherlock (9)
Arden Primary School

IN THE WINTER

If you want this poem to rhyme,
make each word rhyme in each line.
In the winter when snow is deep,
Leaves are lying in a heap.
All of the sheep are nice and warm,
While we are making snowmen and having fun.

Stephanie Sawers (9)
Arden Primary School

BEING HEALTHY

Being healthy is
A big part of life
Being healthy is
Being smart
Eat some beans
They have protein
Eating beans is eating healthily.

Scott MacDonald (9)
Arden Primary School

A MONKEY IN A TREE

A monkey in a tree
That's what I'd like to be
Not a tiger or a chimpanzee
You see, monkeys can climb trees
Really high in the sky
Well, if you really want to be
A tiger or a chimpanzee
Then it's fine with me
But!
I'd rather be a monkey in a tree.

Emma Gallacher (8)
Atholl Preparatory School

WEAK MAN

Weak man is thin
Weak man is light
Weak man has no muscle
Weak man is slow
Weak man has baby power
Weak man is *no good!*

Shuto Fukuyo (8)
Atholl Preparatory School

INJECTIONS

Injections always make me quiver,
They also make me shake and shiver.
When the needle goes near, I shout out and say,
'I'm going! Get out of my way.'

The nurse says, 'No,' and holds me back.
Then she smiles and gives me a Tic-Tac.
Then all at once she put the needle in,
And when she took it out I said,
'I didn't feel a thing.'

Rosalind Philips (8)
Atholl Preparatory School

GIANTS

Some giants are big,
Some giants are small,
Some in between
And some not at all,
I like the ones that are small
Because they won't eat me at all.

Jennifer Sinclair (7)
Atholl Preparatory School

VOYAGE TO SPACE

I wish I could go to space,
Play cards on the rocket,
I've won, I've got an ace.

Fly to Jupiter and Mars!
Eat Milky Way chocolate bars!

But now I'm going home,
I'm getting rather sad,
Missing Mum and Dad.

Amy Douglas (8)
Atholl Preparatory School

ME IN MY BED

Me in my bed all alone,
Except for cat that is fat.
I got out of bed
and knocked on the door,
but Mum didn't come.
I knocked again
and she came.
I said to her I am all alone.
She shut the door and said,
'Go to bed,'
So . . . me in my bed alone.

Lara Davidson (7)
Atholl Preparatory School

THE NIGHT THE MOON WENT RED

On a dark, cold winter's night,
The moon is giving off a silver misty light,
A shining pale glowing face,
Suddenly disappearing without a trace,
All is silent, gloomy and dark,
No birds cheep, no dogs bark,
Wait, it's coming back to take a peek,
Like a silver-faced baby with a rosy cheek.

With all the stars that twinkle above,
I think the red glowing moon resembles love,
Then from red to orange, to yellow, to silver,
Will I live to see this again? Will anyone, ever?
A bright curved line that shines down the lane,
But now it's a bright silver ball again.

Kimberley Grierson (11)
Bargeddie Primary School

MY MUM

My mum has lots of things about her
That I love very much.
When the wind blows towards me,
It's like her gentle touch.

My mum is just a little dear,
When I'm with her, I have no fear.
My problems are gone, they fade away,
My mum she helps me every day.

My mum has a special corner inside
Her heart, reaches out just like the tide.
She'll have my tea ready at 5:00 I'll bet,
'Cause as far as I can see,
She's the best mum you can get.

Kelsey Brown (11)
Bargeddie Primary School

THE VOYAGE OF THE DAMBUSTERS

Vroom, vroom, the engines roar.
Boom, boom, shuts the door.
The pilot gets into gear,
Then the plane he starts to steer.
He then pulls back on the stick,
The plane is up in a tick.

They go over the fields and hills,
The gunner, his gun he fills.
He hears the bullets in the chamber rattle,
Ready for the coming battle.
The crew return with a sigh,
I wonder how many Germans died?

Scott Cullen (11)
Bargeddie Primary School

FESTIVALS

Hallowe'en is a scary night,
And you will probably get a fright.
Ghosts, ghouls and creepy phantoms,
Light up the eerie darkness.
With your orange pumpkin lanterns,
Surrounded by screams.
They will continue to haunt little children's dreams,
But they will go back to bed,
Back to sleep to rest their heads.

Fireworks light up the night sky,
Whooshing up so very high.
The loud bangs may give you a fright,
Twisting, swirling, oh what a sight!
Bonfires crackle as they burn,
Beautiful colours as the catherine wheels turn.
Now they die in the sky,
They come every year for you and I.

These are two main events,
Many children think they're heaven sent.
For me, fireworks night or Hallowe'en,
It's really hard to choose,
They are both great fun,
So I really can't lose!

Robyn Jenkins (11)
Bargeddie Primary School

HALLOWE'EN NIGHT

On Hallowe'en night you'll be in for a fright,
Vampires and witches, they stay up all night.
Witches are wandering up in the air,
Vampires suck blood from every child that's near.

So when you hear a scream beware,
It could be a goblin,
Or a vampire,
Or even a skeleton,
Chasing children everywhere!

Amie McLaughlin (11)
Bargeddie Primary School

MY FRIEND, SONNY

I have a friend called Sonny,
He's very smart and funny,
He always makes me laugh, not cry,
He's never even told me a lie,
He's always there when I'm upset,
He sits beside me and calls me Pet.

Stephanie Campbell (11)
Bargeddie Primary School

STARS

Shining down from the velvet black heaven,
Watching over the world we live in,
A terrific mass
Of flaming gas,
Looking down from the never-ending sky,
Like beautiful, loving, twinkling eyes,
Silently shining with all their might,
To magically light up the cruel, cold night,
Glittering balls of mysterious fire
That seem to know my every desire.

Kirsten Savage (11)
Bargeddie Primary School

MATHS

Maths is rotten,
It's really very bad.
We're taught by Mr Cotton,
He's always very mad!

Who cares what 3x3 is?
I'm only in primary 4.
But I know he gave Miss Washman a kiss,
As she walked out the door!

Ooh, aah, I'm going to tell,
Oh too late, there's the bell.
Maths is over for today,
But tomorrow is another dreaded day!

Donna Wilkinson (10)
Bargeddie Primary School

OCEAN

The ocean is an emerald blanket,
That swirls and flips around.
It jumps and lands with a splat,
To the ocean's watery ground.

The ocean's floor is full of life,
The colours are warm and cold.
Fish are searching for their food,
That seems hopeless to find.

The deep, dark ocean escapes the light.
Crystal water sparkles in daylight.
The ocean is a wonderful place,
Still unspoilt by the human race.

Ross Bell (11)
Bargeddie Primary School

Autumn

One frosty autumn morning,
It's 9 o'clock and I'm still yawning,
Lots of beautiful leaves are around,
Stunning colours, reds and greens lying on the ground.

I like autumn, the best season,
The weather and colours are the reason,
Looking up, the trees they are becoming bare,
Leaves coming down covering the stairs.

Night is starting to fall,
Then I hear my mum call,
I take one last look at the wonderful sight,
Now I have to go, it doesn't seem right!

Robert Totten (11)
Bargeddie Primary School

Colourful Day

When I'm looking at the sky,
The sun is shining bright,
It's reflecting on the water,
Making it look like a sparkling otter.

The sun is still shining,
But the clouds begin to form,
The rain, it starts belting down,
And the rainbow makes a crown.

The rainbow is so colourful,
Like fireworks in the sky,
And I have been told if you are bold,
At the end you will find a pot of gold.

Gemma Cochrane (11)
Bargeddie Primary School

GROWING OLDER

A slabbering baby feeding,
A crying baby teething.
A wee toddler crawling,
A big toddler standing.
A cool child fanning,
A hot child panting.
A worried teenager getting married,
A busy teenager working at college.
An adult playing bingo,
An adult washing the dishes.
An OAP going to the doctor's,
An OAP resting at home.

David Murray (8)
Burnbrae Primary School

VOYAGE OF LIFE

A happy baby sleeping,
A chubby, happy baby giggling,
A yelling toddler greetin',
A quiet toddler crawling.
A hairy child brushing,
A noisy child shouting.
A lively teenager dancing,
A tired teenager sleeping.
A busy adult working,
A tired adult sleeping.
An old pensioner going to the shops,
An old pensioner going to the shops slowly.

Ashley Peacock (8)
Burnbrae Primary School

OUR LIFE'S JOURNEY

A beautiful baby teething,
A happy, funny baby feeding.
A cheeky toddler scratching,
A happy toddler chewing.
A child learning numberwork in maths,
A child good on the computer.
A teenager moaning for make-up,
A teenager out dancing with her friend.
An adult working all week,
An adult out buying all the shopping.
A pensioner sitting in the garden with all the family,
Enjoying a barbecue with everybody.

Nicole Harris (8)
Burnbrae Primary School

THE SMUGGLER

My name is Snakehair,
I am a secret smuggler
Working on the coast,
I am smuggling diamonds and jewels.
I have to be very careful and I feel very brave.
This is my horse,
She is called Black Bess.
She has to carry a heavy load and is very strong.
We have to work quietly and quickly.
Do you think we will be seen?

Amanda Littlejohn (9)
Burnbrae Primary School

VOYAGES

Fly, fly, take me away,
Take me to my destiny.
In this jet, strapped to my seat,
The world goes by as I look through my feet.
I breathe in air, hard and breathless
As I fly high in the sky.

The force of speed blows against my face,
The rumbling of the engine echoes in my ear,
The plane rumbles, then stumbles,
I then lose control.

I get control back . . . but . . .
The fuel is getting low . . . and . . .
The plane is getting slow
It goes down, down, down . . .

I launch the ejector seat
The seat flies . . . but the jet nose dives
I float down, down, down, . . . and
I land safely on the sand.

James Johnston (11)
Burnbrae Primary School

THE WORST VOYAGE OF MY LIFE!

The worst voyage of my life
Was is in January this year,
And you never saw anything like it,
For this time of year.

It became foggy that day
Then the waves became wild
And slapped the ship from side to side
The wind became strong

The sailors worked hard
To save their lives
Then they became seasick
The sky started to disappear from the fog

And it's still happening
Will this day ever end?

Christopher Black (11)
Burnbrae Primary School

THE FLYING ISLAND

The flying island,
The flying island.
The flying island is taking me away,
The flying island is coming your way.

I'm going to Egypt,
I'm going to Tibet.

I'm travelling North,
I'm travelling East, South, West.
But don't forget, I'm coming your way.
See me!
See me!

See me in the sky,
See me under water.
I will be coming some time soon.
This is the beginning,
This is the end.
This voyage will never end,
I guess it's just me.
I'm the Star Voyager!

Nicola Murray (10)
Burnbrae Primary School

GROWING UP

A beautiful, funny baby smiling,
A happy, chubby baby bouncing.
A messy, hyper toddler breaking,
A messy, greedy toddler feeding.
A fit, sporty child exercising,
A hairy, lazy child moaning.
A plooky teenager squeezing,
A smart teenager revising.
A shattered adult working,
A knackered adult baby-sitting.
An ancient OAP limping along,
An OAP proud of them all.

John Buchanan (10)
Burnbrae Primary School

SHIP ON FIRE

I am a strong sailor on the bounty
The fire is burning hotly.
Listen to the crackles
There is smoke all around
People are coughing and spluttering.
I have to be brave.
I have to help the frightened to safety.
The ship will soon go down.
We will have to jump into the cold, icy water.
It is our only chance!

Christopher Dunne (9)
Burnbrae Primary School

SPACE VOYAGE RACE!

We're getting into the rocket
To go way, way up in space.
We're flying in the human V's alien race.
But when we got there
Something terrible went wrong.

We saw a meteorite in front of the sun,
It was heading for Alien V112's ship.
Oh no . . . now he's dead . . . *crash!*
It's heading straight for us.
We must move fast
Or we're going to *blast!*

We started with eleven people,
Now we're only down to one.
I'm sorry to hear about
Alien V112's dad,
But he was going loopy,
He was going mad . . .

Because

Alien V112 is dead . . .
At long, long last!

Jade Reid (11)
Burnbrae Primary School

VOYAGE IN SPACE

Space! Space! I live in space.
I belong to an alien race.

I live on Venus
I live on Mars
I even live
On the hottest stars.

But I can't live on the sun
Because it's far too hot
Or I will just turn into
A great big heat spot!

I know a Martian
He is called Light
It always appears
He wants to fight!

He comes from deep
Of the bottom of space
In fact he belongs to
The *Bazzawazza* race!

It's time, it's time
I go inside.
I have to comb
My *hairy hide!*

Jade Macleod (11)
Burnbrae Primary School

THE VOYAGE

Captain Rook and his crew of five
Went sailing in the Caribbean Sea.
They were heading to the Gulf of Mexico
Then deep into the Atlantic Ocean.

It was a perfect day when
Captain Rook said,
'What a perfect day, it's turned out fine,
I'm glad the weather turned out the way it did!'

By the time the crew reached the Gulf of Mexico
It was cold, it was wet, and it was dark.
Then out of the blue a storm approached
And the captain shouted, 'Get inside!'

It was very rough and the waves were high,
They were glad they were in the harbour.
By the time the storm left, they were off again,
Right into the Atlantic Ocean.

They went on to Cuba, everything was fine,
Nothing was very different.
But the crew of five became the crew of three
With Captain Rook and his shiny hook, although
Why this happened nobody knows!

Marie Dempster (10)
Burnbrae Primary School

MY VOYAGE

When I was four
I knocked on my father's door
He said to me, 'Get to bed!'
I said to him, 'I'll go and see Ed.'

Ed was the captain, he had a dog
His name was Dirty, Dirty Mog.
His bed was made of wooden logs.

It was a dark and windy night
It gave me a great big fright
I said to Mog, 'Hold on tight!'
For soon it was light.

All he did was bark
I think he found it dark
I heard someone shout, 'Help, help!'
It sounded like Ed.

He told me to get my dad . . . and . . .
He looked very mad.

Why?

He was mad because the boat was sinking
He said to me, 'Get Skunk!'
I said, 'That little punk!'

Pamela Howson (10)
Burnbrae Primary School

THE CASTLE

The castle is silent now
Where once there was a row
The castle is silent now
Where knights once marched
Through doors once arched
That is now rubble
Where a traitor got in deep trouble
The castle is silent now
Where horses once trotted
Where a spy was spotted
The castle is silent now
Where swords once clashed
And shields were bashed
The castle is silent now
Where fires burned
And stomachs churned
At the cook's watery stew!

James Elliott (11)
Clober Primary School

TEACHERS

How come teachers who have a brain
Can also be such a pain.
They give you work to do all day
And now with homework there's no time to play.
Sentences, spelling and parent prompts,
This is not what children want.
Teacher, teacher, we should have a say,
Remember what it was like in your day.
Please be kind, I'm only young,
But sadly for P1s the homework has just begun.

Maegan Shearer (11)
Clober Primary School

MY FANTASY WORLD

I am in my own little world,
Just me, that little girl.
I lie on clouds in the sky,
Up there I feel so high.
The clouds are like ice cream,
Oh, what a dream.
I smell chocolate and marshmallows,
I wish it was in barrels.

Most horses canter round and round,
Like our massive roundabout.
I have a castle that is so tall,
Compared to me, I am so small.
It sounds so peaceful and relaxing,
With no phones to go ring, ring.

It smells so clean,
It's even got its own netball team.
I play in it,
I train quite a bit.
Clean air,
With also girls' well-washed hair.
You should come,
You are welcome.

Katie Gourlay (11)
Clober Primary School

PUSSY CAT

Pussy cat, pussy cat on the rug
I feel like giving you a big hug
Your velvet black fur
And your big beady eyes
I could never get a better prize

Pussy cat, pussy cat curled in a ball
You are the best pet of all
Your wagging tail
And your little black paws
I'll love you forever and more!

Chris Stevenson (9)
Clober Primary School

THE SEA STORM

The waves were crashing
like two male stags
for supremacy.

The hungry creatures were
snapping at the boat like bear
traps crunching the unaware prey.

The fish nets were whipping
for fish like a jockey whipping
for a victory in the last fifth.

The seamen were fighting for dear life
as the smashing wind's
toppling the boat like a mighty
giant falling to the ground.

The lightning was flashing
like a giant Catherine wheel
going off at close range,
the thunder was crashing
like Tyson's fist hitting the challenger.

Thomas Matthew (11)
Clober Primary School

SNOOPY

I have a budgie called Snoopy,
I've had him for over three years.
I didn't know what to call him,
And Snoopy came out of the blue.

Snoopy's not thin, but not fat.
His favourite things are his bell and his bath.
He likes flying and eating our pictures,
But most of all biting our fingers.

His beak's as bright as the sunlight,
His breast's as blue as the sky,
He chirps whenever you're near him,
He's quiet whenever you're gone.

He can open the door to his cage.
I think he should be on the stage.

Katie Telfer (11)
Clober Primary School

MY RABBIT

My rabbit has big toes
And likes to jump about in the snow
When you shine the light on her
You can see her red eyes
My rabbit is called Bambi
My rabbit has a sister
They both fight like me and my big sister
Bambi pulls Thumper's fur out.

Kirsty Gray (8)
Clober Primary School

MY FAVOURITE ANIMAL

My favourite animal you'll have to guess
It lives in Africa, leaving its horrible mess
Wherever it goes to get its food
Is never far in this giant wood

I like this animal, its ivory tusks
As it walks through Africa from dawn 'til dusk
Its thick grey hide is course and rough
And in the jungle it has to be tough

My favourite animal, have you guessed yet?
Are you going to place a bet?
The African elephant, one of my favourite creatures
And I have told you its best features.

Ross Taylor (11)
Clober Primary School

LIGHTNING

Crash! Bang! Pow!
The lightning goes in the dark,
Like a little spark.
Blink and you've missed it,
People think it's exquisite,
But very scary too.
Don't stay outside or you'll get shocked,
And shocked you will be when you come too.
You'll be startled and afraid,
How is it made?
By water crystals in the air.
It's 10 times hotter than the sun,
So you'd better *run!*

Douglas Bouttell (11)
Clober Primary School

HOLIDAYS

I love holidays
Getting on the plane
Drinking all the coke I want
Again and again

I love the beach
Sitting in my chair
Wearing a floppy hat
To protect my hair
With cream on my nose
And sand between my toes
I sit and dream
About my next ice cream

I love swimming
Jumping in and out
Wearing my armbands
I'd never do without

I love eating
Going out every night
Choosing chips and pizza
It's my favourite bite

I love going home
All pink and tanned
Start to plan the next one
Before we even land.

Fiona Bain (11)
Clober Primary School

ALPHABET MANIA

A ll Saints are all hooked up
B ritney's stronger than ever
C raig David's walking away
D avid Grey is Babylon
E minem's the real slim shady
F ive slam dunk da funk
G ina G's just a little bit
H eather Small's just what you need
I an Wright wants chicken tonight
J amilia just called me
K ylie Minogue is spinning around
L ouise is two-faced
M adonna's telling me
N -Sync are saying goodbye
O asis saying Sunday morning calls
P ink makes you feel sick
Q ueen's rocking you
R obbie's a rocking DJ
S teps are stomping all night now
T exas have an inner smile
U sher's popping ya collar
V anessa Amorusi is shining
W estlife have a dream
X -Files are spooking you
Y MCA says the Village People
Z ing that song says Bing Crosby
and that's a rap!

Gemma Powell (11)
Clober Primary School

THE PLAYGROUND

In the playground you can see children
Playing hide and seek.
When the children run to hide the
Seeker has to run and find.
When the seeker finds them he
Has to run and say inden.
Some girls like to play with Barbies like Ken.
But boys like to play with Action Men.
Some like watching the green, brown and
Yellow leaves falling off the trees like
Confetti in the strong wind.
The boys and girls like playing on the
See-saw, going up and down like the
Waves in the sea.
While other children like to play on the swings
All day.
But when the bell goes, they have to
Stand up straight and wait for the teacher
To come out at the end of break.

Karen Ferguson (11)
Clober Primary School

ANIMAL CARE

I'm terrible with animals I know
Although it doesn't show

I had four fish for a week
The others I didn't really feed

Don't lend me a pet for a day
It would either die or run away

When I am older I would like a pet
I would take care of it better than the rest

If my cat's a girl, I will call it Twirl
If my cat's a boy, I will call it Troy

Please don't get me wrong, I do like pets
But I can't take care of them as well as the rest.

Mhairi Millar (11)
Clober Primary School

TWISTER

A twister is as fierce as a bulldog,
And as angry as a bear.
If a house gets in its way, you know it's going to tear.
A twister is as loud as a roaring lion,
It's so loud it's hard to believe.
When a twister is coming, you must get into a basement or cellar,
There's nowhere safer than there.
It twirls as fast as a cheetah chasing its prey,
When one's coming it's a good idea to get out of the way.
A twister is so unpredictable you don't know what direction it will go,
North, South, East or West and will you be picked up in its flow.
It grinds items like a piece of metal being dragged along the street,
Nobody really knows what it's found.
Twisters are stronger than ten of the world's strongest men,
They destroy buildings, houses and sheds and nearly all other
                                                        tall structures,
It's as destructive as the huge crushing machines in the junk yard,
And as vicious as a raging bull.
But when it's died down or moved on,
You'll just need to get another or rebuild what was there
                                                        but now gone.

Johnathan McNabb (11)
Clober Primary School

MY DAY

I get up early in the morning
A new day is dawning
Eat cereal, toast, juice for breakfast
I'd better be quick or I'll
Get to the bathroom last.

I walk slowly to school
And see the girls drool
Sums, language, gym
And topics take up the day
I hurry home quickly
And go out to play.

I play football and chappie
My mum was not happy!
I eat jam on bread
And go early to bed.

Scott Roger (11)
Clober Primary School

THE SNOW

I went outside today
And the snow was all away
I made snowballs yesterday
I can't make them today
I wish the sun went away
And snow came again
The snow is good to play in
The sun is hot and flaring
I don't like it when it thaws
I wish the snow came back!

James Crane (8)
Clober Primary School

THE OLYMPICS

The Olympics are held every four years,
It started in Athens in Greece,
Competitors get to hold the Olympic torch,
And one gets to light the flame,
The Millennium Games were held in Sydney,
There was the swimming and track and field.
No one could run like Maurice Green,
'Cause he's the fastest in the world.
There are many sports to play,
To try and grab a gold, silver or bronze.
You have to train very hard to win,
But even just to race is a big part.

Ross Byford (11)
Clober Primary School

SAILING IN SPACE

Hoist the sails
We're passing Mars today
We're going to Venus tomorrow
So get on deck I say

Scrub the decks
Turn the ship into Mars
Hurry it up!

Look at the other planets
Thinking where we're going next
I know we're going
To Venus but where next?

Mark Welsh (9)
Clober Primary School

BUBBLEGUM

I like blowing bubbles with bubblegum
Then popping them with my thumb

I prefer Bazooka the best
As it blows bigger bubbles than all the rest

I collect wrappers called 'Bazooka Joe the Radio Man'
And I get bubblegum as often as I can

When I go to the shops
I buy lots

To satisfy my taste
And in case it goes to waste

So much bubblegum has touched my tongue
That I'm surprised it's not got stuck in my lungs.

Kyle Buchanan (11)
Clober Primary School

JOURNEY TO THE MAGIC MOON

I'm looking out the window
I see the open space
It is scary when craters come bouncing at you
It is so quiet but I am sure
I heard something turn around to face me
I see the magic moon
But when I turn the Earth is there
The moon seems magic but
Earth has cut down trees!

Craig Williamson (9)
Clober Primary School

THE EGYPTIAN SUN

The day has just begun and the warm dry
Sand is becoming clear as the sun draws so near
The sun has just filled the sky with the heat
Spreading all around and when you look up
You see that beautiful golden nugget up high in the sky

The mid-afternoon has appeared now, the sun seems
So near and we look all around and see how the
Nile spreads right down with its guardian the sun and
Its creator RA!

Now the sun has shone and gone. The moon
Shines over the dark, crisp sand. But all is not
Over yet because that tan of gold has risen
Once again and we all call it . . .
Egyptian Sun.

Robbie Grey (9)
Clober Primary School

SHIP

You're sailing, we're watching
When you're sleeping we'll be sailing till dawn
When you get up there will be a ship
You will sail around the world with sailors and across the Seven Seas
Then say the word
Fly then fly and fly till you get to the other side
Don't worry for now the ship will protect you
When you come back we will have a feast.

Craig Purdie (9)
Clober Primary School

MY SQUASH CAR

My big squash car
Zooms around the road

He can run and skip
And hop as well, just like a toad

The rackets coming out of him
Can hit small balls

And if you crash into them
He won't be hurt at all

He's a squash world champion
He's beaten all the rest

My big squash car
I think he's the best

When he dies he'll go to heaven
Because he came from a place called Devon.

Scott Watson (9)
Clober Primary School

SEASONS

Winter brings the snow
And summer makes it glow
Autumn brings the fall
Spring brings the lambs that sit on the wall
All these seasons bring a different thing
But I like it best when the birds sing
My birthday's in May
So was my gran's but she passed away.

Ross Easton (9)
Clober Primary School

RAINY DAYS

Today was a wet and rainy day,
my mum says I am not allowed out to play.

I stood standing looking out of the window
for a very long time,
there were very big raindrops coming
from the stop sign.

I went upstairs to play with my toys,
then the doorbell rang, I ran down the stairs,
it was my best friend with
her Winnie the Pooh toys.

We had such fun,
my mum shouted up,
'There is the sun.'

So my friend Helen and I
came running down the stairs,
but the rain was still raining cats and dogs.

Fiona Dickson (9)
Clober Primary School

SPACEMAN

The shuttle started, *boom!*
It went to space and back again,
The shuttle went past Venus and over
Stars and Mars.

Saturn is the place for me and
I went for tea,
The shuttle started off, I went back
To Earth again.

Mark Saunders (9)
Clober Primary School

THE SNAKE

It slithered along the leaves,
It slithered on people's sleeves,
Injecting a poisonous venom
Into their knees,
Then he simply slithers back
In among the leaves of the jungle,
He lays out his long tail,
Searching along the jungle floor,
For what seems to be his dinner
Is simply just an egg,
'Aha,' he says, 'I've found my egg.'
And he gobbles it up in one big bite.
'That's a day's work,' he says,
And then he goes back to sleep.

Scott Maxwell (11)
Clober Primary School

WINTER WONDERLAND

I just love it
in the winter when
snow falls but does
not splinter

Children rush
outside to play
and cheer for
the snowy day

And all around us
blows the blizzard
that has been put
there by a wizard.

Amy Louise Hendry (8)
Clober Primary School

PETS

Fun to have but cost to keep,
They come in different sizes,
Small, big and medium,
They are fluffy, bald, long-haired and scaled,
Live in water and cages,
Some run mad about
The house chasing things,
Hamsters stuffing food in their pouches
And Dalmatians having to be walked
Every three hours,
Cats wandering about the streets,
Hungry dogs barking at the door
When someone rings it,
Rats they have long tails,
Furry coats, they run on wheels
When they wake up,
Pets, they come in all colours,
Black, white, spotted
And brown and grey,
Pets, fun to have, cost to keep.

Mark Bohonek (11)
Clober Primary School

HERE COMES THE SNOW

Here comes the snow
Falling down in wee bits
People running out building snowmen
Dressing like snowmen with hats and scarves
Kids going down the hill in sledges
Shaking the trees for snow.

Greig Roger (9)
Clober Primary School

ANIMALS

Maybe you have a cat
Even a mouse or rat
With big brown eyes or a fluffy tail
A big black dog or a silver snail.

I have a fish that swims in a tank
With goggly eyes and a big orange tail
Would you like to swim with a dolphin
Or dive like a whale?

Hop like a rabbit in long strands of grass
Or be like a crab with a shell of brass,
Fly like a bird from tree to tree,
Or eat from the flowers like a big buzzing bee.

Hang on the trees like a koala bear
Be as bright as a lizard with colourful hair
As small as a frog
Or a working ant building in logs
Or a lovely big playful golden dog.

Perhaps you would like a rabbit
With a tail like cotton wool
Ears to hear, when the birds glide down
Big feet to hop from burrow to burrow
Or dig from time to time
Any of these I wouldn't mind.

Nicola Raworth (10)
Clober Primary School

MY RATS

Curled up in bed
Mostly in a cage
Let them out occasionally
Sometimes on the move

Two handfuls of food is all they need
Straight in there head first
Eating only bit by bit

Wakes me up at twelve o'clock
Slurping mouths of water down
And jumping different obstacles
Squeaking as they go

Their tails are full of muscle
And curl up to their muzzle
To feel them it soothes me
But most people flee
But there is nothing to be afraid about
It's only hairy skin

Thank God my mum was there
To back me up if not
I would not have
My two beautiful rats

But even though they wake me up or disturb me
My rats and I have a friendship forever!

Calum Shaw (11)
Clober Primary School

TITANIC

Mr Ismay knew she was unsinkable
Mr Andrew's not too sure
All her passengers believed
They were all soon to know
The ship they called unsinkable
Could sink like a ten ton weight

The ninety nine foot 'berg
Punctured holes along her like Morse code
The steering locked up
The rich let out
Water leaked in
People began to drown

Lifeboats were lowered
Rockets were fired
Passengers in distress
Screaming on decks
While officers man the boats

The bow went down
And stern rose up
The band kept playing
No matter what
The ship plunged
To the ocean floor
Killing a thousand and many more.

Richard Pollock (11)
Clober Primary School

HOLIDAY

When we arrive at Glasgow Airport
We get on a plane and fly
Up in the sky
I see the clouds that are white
And fluff just like a McFlurry

    We arrive on the ground
    In a hurry
    And you can hear the tyres squeak!
    When we came out
    It was hot and sunny
    Without a cloud in the sky

We grab our luggage and rush in a hurry
Just to catch a cab
We arrive at the hotel to unpack
'Come on Mum and Dad! I'm hungry'
We stuffed our faces with pizza
Now it's time to go exploring
We visit the sights and shows
Oh what a day

    We go to the theme parks
    And ride the rollercoasters
    We eat all we want
    We see the stars and watch the water shows
    Sadly it's time to go.

Jason McCabe (11)
Clober Primary School

THERE IS A PLACE

There is a place
Where men and women go
But it is not a holiday, O Lord, no,
In this place
No Sun,
Just rain,
For this is not an evil place,
But a place where evil people go,
For they have done what we call crime.

You get up at seven,
Not a quarter to eleven
And get to work on cleaning the floor.
Or worse, worse more,
The warden's door,
Who's more like God,
Until you leave or die.

In this place,
You don't know
Who to trust or why to leave,
For you're all in disgrace,
Some murderers,
Some thieves
And some of you might not leave this place.

There is a thing
Called the electric chair,
Which all four
And some draw near
To sitting in old sparkey's lap
And when you're on there's no escape
From this place except going to heaven.

Gary Hutchison (11)
Clober Primary School

ONE GOOD FOOTBALLER

Once there was a footballer, he stepped on the pitch
and he had no fear like a musketeer.

He goes to play football on a sunny day like he
does every Saturday.

While he is going barmy in his Ferrari as his team
won 3-1 today and he got three goals and they
all hit off the poles.

His wages shot up to 40,000 pounds a week
because he was Greek.

He got injured and it hurt and all of his blood
went splurt because someone's stud went into his leg.

Daryl Bell (9)
Clober Primary School

WORLD WAR TWO

W orld War 2, violence and booming has just begun,
O nce again like screaming World War 1
R acing, rumbling, charging ahead,
L oved ones worry if their husbands are dead
D ashing, charging, raging ahead to fight

W hen in the black-out there must be no light
A nnoyed and raging mothers you can hear
R aging as their children get moved to nowhere near

T rashing the city with booming bombs
W orld War 2 is as buzzing as ever, this is Hitler's fault
O nce again I ask, when will this firing mess end?

Miriam McKay (10)
Corpus Christi Primary School

SURVIVAL

Dreaming soundly under a thick blanket
Hugging a favourite teddy of mine
Seeing enchanted people from places beyond
In my dreams.
Speckles of rain upon my windowsill.
Swishing cars fly past outside
Their light illuminating my bedroom
I feel safe here.

Deep sound rising in pitch
Disturbing my slumber
Higher, higher, my body shakes in fear
Insistent noises shrieking.
The siren.
My eyes open.

Springing out of bed,
Scurrying and grabbing my leaving bag.
Comforting my pet,
Saying goodbye
We run for safety.
Terrifying bombs flying from the night sky
Ammunition being fired off
Worrying about my pet.
Silence falls.

Pushing open the shelter door
Bitter smells drift inside
Poor guinea pig found dead
House smashed to the ground.
Shocked at the damage by German bombers
We stand amazed.

Feeling destroyed as my pet guinea pig is found dead.
Happy as the rest of my family is alive
Hearing ambulance sirens now
Coming to the rescue
We have survived.

Jennifer Scott (10)
Corpus Christi Primary School

WORLD WAR TWO

W orld war is back again, crying, zooming, firing, banging
O ffice workers become fire-fighters, fighting back the fire
R inging all around are children screaming and mothers weeping
L ong days pass with roofs normally crumbling in and people shouting
                                                                              from outside
D ads away fighting in a different country during the war

W hy does the war have to be so frightful and violent?
A dolf Hitler is behind all of this plundering
R ow is with Hitler and our government, why are they fighting?
                                                                             asked one little girl

T ick, tock, tick, tock goes the timer for the next bomb
W hat shall we do now, our country has been destroyed!
O h, I can't wait until World War Two is over.

Catherine MacMillan (10)
Corpus Christi Primary School

THIS ROARING WAR

W hy did this man make us want to scream and cry?
O ut go the young men to go to the thundering war
R oaring of the planes makes me very scared
L eaving of the children makes the mothers shout and cry
D aring soldiers risk their lives for us as the thumping tanks go by

W hy does Adolf Hitler laugh and laugh as he bombs us with
                                                          loud bangs
A ll the mothers wail for their little ones' lives
R inging of the sirens makes me want to hide!

T he booming of the bombs makes us all cry
W hy is this happening? The little one said loudly
O h, I hate this booming, roaring war, it's shattering our lives.

Jane Harrison (10)
Corpus Christi Primary School

WORLD WAR TWO

W e remember the memories of the booming world war
O h, why is there so much booming and pouncing?
R oaring of the planes as they came closer
L ouder and louder the firing came
D own came the whizzing planes pounding their bombs

W ailing of the evacuees going away
A gainst the Germans, pounding they were
R emembered is the death toll of the last world war

T humping of the soldiers, shouted in the horizon
W hy did Hitler plunder the world?
O h, why was the war so violent and booming?

Anthony Hughes (10)
Corpus Christi Primary School

WINTER SCENE

Powdery, soft snow on bald, brown trees.
A small castle sitting lonely in the bleak country.
The soft gentle sound of snowflakes falling.
My footsteps in the crunchy tight-packed snow.
The dark dampness of the hills.
My numb fingers stiffen and freeze.

Caroline Maxwell (10)
Corpus Christi Primary School

AMANDA

There once was a girl called Amanda,
all of her friends called her 'Manda.
She had curly hair
and looked like a bear
and they all thought she was a panda.

Amanda Fraser (10)
Drumry Primary School

LOVE

L ove is the most precious thing in the world
O h, how I love my friends.
V ery important friends are to me,
E xcept when I go in a huff.

Kevin Clark (10)
Drumry Primary School

FORGOTTEN

'Be quiet up there!' shouted my mum
I said I was only dancing.
She said I was like an elephant!
How dare she?

'Stop singing in there!' shouted my dad,
I replied I was only practising.
He said I was like an awful cats' choir!
How dare he?

'Why can't you shut up?' I said to them both,
Oh - uh, I done it then.
I blurted out, 'Sorry!'
Then I ran up to my room.

That night at dinner I was nervous,
But my mum and dad were fine!
I thought that they were still angry,
How wrong I was.

I asked my mum if she was angry,
She just laughed and said, 'No!'
Again, I said I was sorry,
She said, 'It's forgotten!'

Then, I asked my dad,
He said, 'It's OK!'
We all had pudding.

It was forgotten in five minutes.

Ashleigh Wilson (11)
Drumry Primary School

ME AND MY MATES

Me and my mates Christopher and Derek,
We hate Digimon because it's pathetic.
We like Pokémon best of all
And sometimes girls, 'cause they're the ball.

We like to have fun,
But only in the hot sun.
We hate the cold,
But when we think of girls we get so hot!
And when we think of some of them we get goosebumps!
Arrgghh!

Barrie Davidson (11)
Drumry Primary School

EMOTIONS

Love is a lovely emotion
it fills your heart with a
soft, cuddly potion.

Sadness, sadness can often lead to badness.

Happiness, happiness, a joyful feeling,
I think that it's a wonderful feeling.

Hate, hate can lead to your fate
and I often think it's a
waste of emotion.

Thomas Curran (11)
Drumry Primary School

MY LITTLE SISTER

M oaning all through the night so you can't get off the light
Y es that's right!

L ittle she may be, annoying as can be
I t's terrible in the house because she can be very loud
T alking is all she really does especially in the house
T alk all day and all night never really puts up a fight
L ittle her mouth may be, but how very loud she can be
E asy life with her around, no way!

S leeping, not such a thing in my house, especially when she's around
I n school she might be good, only if she's in a good mood
S isters can sometimes be good but still very annoying
T hough my sister is a pain I still like her
E very night I'm very tired
R esting we are now, just because she's out!

Stephanie Siller (11)
Drumry Primary School

TEACHERS

Teachers are great!
Teachers are amazing!

Teachers help you with your work!
Teachers help you when you're stuck!

Teachers are great!
Teachers are amazing!

When the teacher is away,
What will we do without her?

Wendy Sharpe (11)
Drumry Primary School

LIFE

Life is strong, worrying,
short and long,
happy, exciting, colourful
and wrong.
Life is different to other stuff,
I can find it easy, hard or sometimes rough.

Work, school, nursery or bed,
wherever you are, life's at the 'B'-ack of your head.
Crying, laughing, here or gone,
life just can go on and on.

Life can mean a lot of things,
but first you've got to know,
that some day or another,
'Life has got to go!'

Karina Duncanson (11)
Drumry Primary School

SPRING

Spring, spring, is a wonderful thing,
all the chicks hatch from their eggs,
little dogs learn to walk on their legs.
The grass turns green and grows very long,
all animals are happy because their babies are born.
Every time you think of spring then you know
it is such a wonderful thing.

Jamielee Downie (10)
Drumry Primary School

MY TEACHER

My teacher Mrs Ayton,
She sometimes shouts
Very loud,
Sometimes I wish,
I wasn't about.

Sometimes she laughs
About things we say,
But she laughs
Mostly all day.

She gave us a present
At Christmas time,
I had forgotten to get her a present,
It must have just slipped my mind.

When she was sick,
She never came to school,
I felt sorry for her,
I really did.

I've had her twice,
In primary four and seven,
She was really nice,
I wished I got her more,
Even though she is my normal teacher.

Sometimes she can be moany,
So I sit and say to myself
Moan, moan, moan, whinge, whinge, whinge
That's all she ever does.

But most of all
She's the best,
Throughout Drumchapel!
She definitely is!

Ashleigh Hinson (11)
Drumry Primary School

WOLF IN THE NIGHT

Wolf in the night,
its howl is so loud,
it scares the village
and the endless crowds.

People are scared
and filled with fright,
children whimper,
for they're scared of the wolf in the night.

Morning dawns, the sun is bright,
the village is safe
from the wolf in the night.

He'll be back when night comes,
when the full moon is bright,
beware of the wolf in the night.

Jamie Sweeney (10)
Drumry Primary School

I WILL MISS . . .

I will miss my mum
Especially in the morning
I'll miss the smell that always comes
When the day is dawning
Also I will miss my friends
But I know that will never end
Just now I'm listening very carefully
To see what I can hear
Cars, trains, lorries, my destination's very near
I'll miss the morning food
That won't be very good
I can almost taste in my mouth
What it's going to be like down South

I'll be seeing my mum
In my head
And be wishing that I
Were in my own bed
I'll be hearing my foster parents talking
It's nice there I suppose
I'll smell the flowers outside
Inside a smell of rose
I will be tasting freedom
But also feeling glum
Because back home where the war is
There also is my mum.

Craig Edwardson (11)
Eastfield Primary School

EVACUATION

Early in the morning we get evacuated,
Very easily we go to the station,
After saying goodbye to my friend,
Casting the bell,
My mum is holding my hand before I go,
After my friend, cheering me away,
The train is starting to go away now,
I'm leaving now,
On the train we go,
No children were ill.

Craig McDonald (12)
Eastfield Primary School

GREAT EXPECTATIONS

Wonderful work
Magnificent maths
Amazing art
Fantastic football
Printing projects
Fascinating French
Exhilarating homework
Outstanding PE
Brilliant monitors
Extraordinary reading
Happy helping.

Chloe Hunter (11)
Eastfield Primary School

EVACUATION

Standing at the station, waiting to be sent away to the country to live with strangers, is what I've always dreaded.

I am only one of the thousands of crying children I can see in the station.

The deafening screech of the whistle blows.

The smell of the musty station and unwashed children surround me.

In one hand I am holding my little sister's shaking hand and in the other, my big, brown label-covered suitcase.

I choke on the train's fumes.

I am sad and scared as we are called into the steam train.

I will miss my family.

Sarah Falconer (10)
Eastfield Primary School

GREAT EXPECTATIONS

A great trip
hard work
troublesome tables
complex computer work
terribly terrific teacher
mean monitors
real responsibilities
bothersome books
cool reading buddies.

Ross Johnston (11)
Eastfield Primary School

EVACUATION

E very time I heard a noise, the noise was of crying
V ery scared faces surrounded me
A nd I can smell and taste the fumes in the air
C hildren and adults devastated, hoping they'd see their family again
U nsolved puzzles for the children that are too young to know
                                              why they are leaving
A result that could leave the world in pain
T ill now an effect that leaves the town in tears
I n every child's heart the hope for life has gone
O n the train as I wave goodbye, I feel my parents' hand through
                                              the narrow window one last time
N ow that life is about to change, a memory that I will never forget.

Megan Greene (11)
Eastfield Primary School

EVACUATION

The station is where my nightmare begins,
Tearful faces begging to stay,
The smell of mustiness surrounds me,
Crying and sobbing is all I can hear,
The taste of fear is overpowering,
I grip my mother's hand even tighter, never wanting to let go,
Heartbroken as the train pulls out.

Louise Warden (11)
Eastfield Primary School

EVACUATION

E vacuation has been announced
V ery frightened faces spread around the country
A s children pack their suitcase with very few things
C hildren standing in the station
U pset children as the parents tell them to go
A chocolate bar was all they got for the journey
T ightly they grip their parents' hands
I nto the train the parents tell them again
O nto the train thousands of children went
N ext they all hope to get a happy family.

Ryan Maginess (11)
Eastfield Primary School

EVACUATION

In one hand my mother's hand and in the other my teddy
And all around me I see bodies, some of which smell.
Everywhere I look I see strangers so I clutch my mother's hand
Tighter than before.
I choke on the fumes as I say bye to my friends.
Sobbing and crying I get on the train.
The whistle goes loud and clear and off we go.
I feel lonely and
I hope I see my family again.

Nikki Andrew (11)
Eastfield Primary School

EVACUATION

E vacuation has begun
V acuees crying as they leave their parents
A s I walk towards my train I shout, 'Goodbye'
C arrying our suitcases and gas mask box
U pset, waving goodbye, parents cry
A rmy troops get ready to go to war
T ension starts as war begins
I am very scared as I leave the station
O ff we go to the countryside
N ow I don't know when I'll see my mum again.

Fiona Dalrymple (11)
Eastfield Primary School

GREAT EXPECTATIONS

An exciting trip
Hard work
Fabulous French
Frenzied football training
Breathtaking PE
Arty art work
Reading buddies
Complex computer work
Helpful RE
Interesting projects
Being monitors
And homework!

Stuart Kearney (11)
Eastfield Primary School

EVACUATION

E very child cries and sobs as they leave their family
V aluable memories left behind
A ccording to my friend it was agonising pain
C an't believe the pain I went through
U nhappy parents leave their children alone in a train station
A bandoned and alone, confused and puzzled they are left with
                                                                these thoughts
T error struck as the train pulled out of the station
I was alone, no sister or family left to comfort me
O h, the pain we went through
N ot one child would forget this memory.

Martina Salveta (11)
Eastfield Primary School

EVACUATION

When I arrive at the station, I begin to get very afraid,
There are hundreds of children surrounding me.
The rusty railtracks seem to go on forever,
There is a horrible smell of unwashed children.
I don't want to let go of my suitcase,
The smoking trains go thundering past.
I can taste the fear in my mind,
Finally the train leaves and takes me into the distance.

Douglas Morton (11)
Eastfield Primary School

EVACUATION

E verywhere crying children and adults alike
V ery sad this time is
A dults everywhere saying goodbye
C hugger chugger goes the train
U ntil we get there, we wonder will we like the family we get
A fter four hours
T he place we're going still unknown
I n the carriage, growing restless
O ther people now come in
N ow finally we get there.

Alan Stewart (11)
Eastfield Primary School

EVACUATION

E vacuation, I'm all ready
V ery sad to leave home
A fter saying goodbye
C ome and see me
U nderstand
A fter the cheering
T he train has gone
I have left
O n the train we go
N o, I want to stay.

Ross Cook (11)
Eastfield Primary School

EVACUATION

E vacuees are all around, all are
V ery scared,
A dolf might attack,
C hildren are taken somewhere
U nknown and they might not come back
A ll the children are on the train
T heir tears do not fade, the train
I s at its destination
O ff they go with their little faces, to a
N ew family they don't even know.

Natalie Fleming (11)
Eastfield Primary School

EVACUATION

The train station is where my sad story begins,
Hundreds of scared and confused faces,
I'm standing here, clutching my mum and dad's hand,
With the stench of smoke, piping around us,
I taste the tears rolling down my face,
There's the whistle, I have to go,
I hope when I come back, I've still got a home.

Neil Buncow (11)
Eastfield Primary School

EVACUATION

My nightmare begins here in the station,
Where there are many frightened faces.
The unwashed children give off a pong,
I can taste the choking fumes.
The whistling trains make me jump,
But I'm safe in my mummy's warm, cosy arms,
That's where I want to stay.
I never want to leave, I'm very, very scared.

Amy Pollock (11)
Eastfield Primary School

EVACUATION

E vacuation has started
V ery, very fast
A thousand parents leave their
C hildren at the station
U pset children
A s they go on the train
T he train
I s about to go
O ff we go, said the driver
N obody was sad on the train.

David Colquhoun (11)
Eastfield Primary School

EVACUATION

E verywhere I look, I can see scared faces
V ery upset parents
A fraid their children might get bombed
C uddling them very tight
U ntil their faces go red
A gonising to watch
T urning my head
I ndeed, everything is sad
O n platform 14c
N ightmare, go, go away.

Keith Sinclair (11)
Eastfield Primary School

PLUTO

P luto is the smallest planet
L ike the moon
U ranus is Pluto's second neighbour
T he moon is about the size of Pluto
O n Pluto you would not survive.

Mark Rodgers (9)
Garthamlock Primary School

SPACE

V enus is the second planet
E arth is its neighbour
N obody lives on Venus
U nlike our planet Earth
S un makes Venus the hottest planet.

Ashleigh Mitchell (9)
Garthamlock Primary School

MERCURY

M ercury is the first planet
E arth is the planet I'm on
R ockets can visit some planets
C onstellations make pictures in the sky
U ranus is a big green planet
R emember that you live on Earth
Y ou can go up into space in a rocket.

Patricia McGonagle (9)
Garthamlock Primary School

PLANETS

P lanets are big and wee
L unar bases are made here
U ranus is quite wee
T he smallest planet is Pluto
O range is the colour of Jupiter.

James MacLeod (9)
Garthamlock Primary School

ORBIT

O rbiting the sun we do
R ockets zooming through and through
B ig, big rockets
I t is really cool
T oo bad we can't see it for real.

Christopher Murphy (9)
Garthamlock Primary School

SPACE

E arth is the third planet from the sun
A steroid belt separate the outer and inner planets
R eally big planets are Jupiter and Saturn
T here are nine planets
H igh up in the solar system.

Alexander Campbell (9)
Garthamlock Primary School

SPACE LIMERICK

There was once a young boy from Mars
Who always looked at the stars
He loved to have fun
And loved eating buns
Especially those made from Mars bars.

Jordan McGlinchey (9)
Garthamlock Primary School

ASHLEY'S POEM ON SPACE

There was once a young boy from Mars
Who loved to play his guitars
He loved to have fun
And look at the sun
And enjoyed eating huge chocolate bars
And he could eat the whole of Mars.

Ashley Andrews (9)
Garthamlock Primary School

HOW TO RIDE A BIKE

First I put my leg over the bike
Then I sit on my saddle
I put my left foot on the pedal
Then I put my right foot on the pedal
Now I am ready to ride my bike
First I must put on my helmet
Then make sure I am safe
Then I put my hands on the handlebars
Then I move my legs to ride the bike
Always watch the road for other traffic
Stay safe on your bike at all times.

Barry Milligan (10)
Holmlea Primary School

THE BEACH

In cool blue sea
There was a lonely fish
Dreaming of a friend to come

Under the golden sand
There was a sad jellyfish
Hoping for a happy day to come

Through the sunny sky
Flew a greedy seagull
Eager for food to come.

Isla Dundas (10)
Holmlea Primary School

IF

If my dad was a pot of paint
He would be a bright, sunny yellow
Happy and cheery, never sad.

If my dad was a bird
He would be a wise little owl
Helping me with all my problems.

If my dad was an animal
He would be a cat.
Soft and gentle always comforting
 me when I'm sad.

If my dad was a flower
He would be a sunflower
Big and bright, always standing tall.

Lynsey Ferguson (9)
Holmlea Primary School

THERE WAS A GIRL WHO TRIPPED

There was a girl who tripped
'Twas like a falling building
When the building was built up again
'Twas like a massive pencil
When the pencil was sharpened
'Twas like a soldier's spear
When the soldiers marched along
'Twas like an army of ants
When the ants piled up in a heap
'Twas that, that tripped the girl.

Anna Papadaki (10)
Holmlea Primary School

THE BOY WHO BRUSHED HIS TEETH

There was a boy who brushed his teeth
'Twas like the bees buzzing around
When the bees stopped
'Twas like a car skidding to a halt
When the car started back
'Twas like a cheetah chasing its prey
When the prey was caught
'Twas like a boy chewing his sweets
When the boy had finished
'Twas like a boy turning off his electric toothbrush.

Jamie Cameron (10)
Holmlea Primary School

AUTUMN GARDENS

Under a bare tree
Yellow leaves are flying
Dancing all around

Under the leaves
A fierce army of ants
Marching towards a pond

Seeds are spreading
Frogs are jumping
All around

On top of the sheds
Brown leaves, yellow leaves
Spreading all around.

Craig Miller (11)
Holmlea Primary School

APPLE

First pick up
Then rub on jumper
See vibrant colours
Shiny all over

Take a bite
Smooth and shiny
Let the flavours go round mouth
Round and round

Let summer flavours come
Vibrant and fresh
Juicy and crunchy
Like the Caribbean

Then swallow it
Feel it go down
Smooth and runny
Very tasty

Take another one

And do it again.

Angus Kean (10)
Holmlea Primary School

IF

If my dad was an animal
He'd be a fox
Cunning and clever always
One step ahead.

If my dad was a bird
He would be a wise owl
Looking down on me
Giving me advice.

If my dad was a pot of paint
He would be bright red
Like a volcano never
Knowing when he's
Going to erupt.

Danny Leinster (9)
Holmlea Primary School

IN MY HEAD AT MATHS TIME

12 + 12, Boring! Boring! Boring!
This is what should be happening:
Radioactive bombs going off in school,
Alarming pupils, creating havoc,
Ill, angry and tired teachers run to the chemistry lab,
Sleeping and snoring, naughty Norman doesn't realise,
Awoken now he laughs cheekily,
Head teacher's office is Norman's new class (probably home),
Detention finishes soon with a fire bell,
For naughty Norman could not cease,
Rackits running again,
Pupils at lunch do not move,
The dinner lady drops bread pudding, starting a food fight,
Children starting to wrench their lunch,
Meanwhile naughty Norman prepares pranks,
Slime, goo and old milk go in,
In the waiting room Norman sniggers,
In comes Miss Melancholy,
Splat! A jelly and custard surprise,
Turn to p16!
Teacher right in front of me now,
So now I know what goes on in my head at
Maths time in detention!

Raisah Din (10)
Holmlea Primary School

IF

If my mum was a pot of paint
She'd be pale blue
Loving and caring for anyone
   in her path.

If my mum was a bird
She'd be a robin
Kind and warm-hearted
   always ready to help.

If my mum was an animal
She'd be a fluffy black and
   white cat
Very kind and gentle
   looking after her kittens

If my mum was a flower
She'd be a bluebell
Pretty, making friends
   with everyone she meets.

Heather Archibald (10)
Holmlea Primary School

WHEN I SAT IN THE AEROPLANE

Z   oom went the aeroplane
U   ruguay was our destination
B   ags were full of clothes that I had on my lap
A   s we were about to land I looked out of the window
I   saw the beautiful country
R   eassured was I of my holiday choice.

Zubair Aslam (11)
Holmlea Primary School

IF

If my mum was a pot of paint
She would be orange
Bright and colourful, always
   cheerful and happy

If my mum was a bird
She would be a parrot
Chatty, finding lots of ways
   to have fun

If my mum was an animal
She would be a Dalmatian
Jumping into everyone's life

If my mum was a flower
She would be a tulip
Throwing her petals to
   anyone who needs her help.

Emma Andrew (9)
Holmlea Primary School

LADY DAISY

L   ittle Lady Daisy lived in
A   small town
D   own by a
Y   acht in London

D   aft Ned found Lady Daisy
A   t his grandmother's house
I   n a box up in the attic
S   he must have been in that box for
Y   ears and years.

Darren Ashton (10)
Holmlea Primary School

IF

If my mum was a pot of paint
She'd be light green
Soft like grass, brightening up the day.

If my mum was a bird
She'd be an owl
Full of wisdom, always there for you.

If my mum was an animal
She'd be a cat cuddling up in front of the fire
After a hard day's work.

If my mum was a flower
She'd be a daffodil
Bright and cheerful when the day is grey.

Emma Lee (9)
Holmlea Primary School

LADY DAISY

L ittle did Ned know he was going to find
A doll called Lady Daisy who was
D azzling with long black hair and looked so
Y oung and pretty in her apple green gown

D own to her ankles with little flowers and
A pink sash and shoes and to think of her
I n a shoe box neatly tied up with
S tring it made him want to cry, she had been there
Y ears and years without knowing.

Fiona Young (10)
Holmlea Primary School

IF

If my mum was a pot of paint
She'd be sunshine yellow
Lighting up our family like the sun.

If my mum was a bird
She'd be a wise owl
Helping me with all my problems.

If my mum was an animal
She'd be a Scottish terrier
Rubbing her white fur against cheerful people.

If my mum was a flower
She'd be a tulip
Purple and lilac opening up in the summer sun.

Saimah Din (9)
Holmlea Primary School

HAIKU POETRY

On the shed rooftop
The bluebird singing loudly
Beside a tall tree.

The leaves are falling
Slowly off a chestnut tree
Onto the soft grass.

In the compost heap
A thousand beetles marching
Through the mighty town.

Scott Fulton (10)
Holmlea Primary School

If

If my sister was a pot of paint
She would be a beautiful light blue
Showing her kindness to her friends and family.

If my sister was a bird
She would be a bright peacock
Showing off the latest fashion
With her fancy clothes.

If my sister was an animal
She would be a llama, always grumpy
When she doesn't get her way.

If my sister was a flower
She would be a beautiful red rose
Blooming in the sun filling the
Air with a sweet smell of happiness.

Graeme Smart (9)
Holmlea Primary School

If

If my grandpa was a pot of paint
He'd be blue like the sky or the deep blue sea
Calming everyone when they are worried or upset.

If my grandpa was a bird
He'd be a wise old owl
Telling me the answers
To all the things I don't know.

If my grandpa was an animal
He'd be a fluffy white cat
All cosy in bed, making friends
Purring on my lap.

If my grandpa was a flower
He'd be a bright yellow sunflower
Just like the sun
Happy, kind and friendly every day.

Emma Strickland (9)
Holmlea Primary School

IF

If my mum was a pot of paint
She would be a bright pink
Loving and caring.

If my mum was a bird
She would be a parrot
Chatty and friendly.

If my mum was an animal
She would be a Dalmatian dog
Kind and cheerful to everyone.

If my mum was a flower
She would be a red rose
Shining in the sunlight
Bringing happiness to the world.

Lee McColl (9)
Holmlea Primary School

IF

If my grandpa was a pot of paint
He would be a glowing gold
Lighting up the dark, keeping me safe.

If my grandpa was a bird
He would be a blackbird
Swooping down, catching a worm
  and swallowing it in one go.

If my grandpa was an animal
He would be a guard dog
Protecting me from evil.

If my grandpa was a flower
He would be a bright sunflower
Cheering everyone up as he went along.

Lee Clark (9)
Holmlea Primary School

THERE WAS A GIRL WHO . . .

There was a girl who brushed her teeth
'Twas like a milkshake full of froth
When the milkshake spilt over
'Twas like a murky river spilling out
When the river ran down the road
'Twas like the car was a little boat
When the boat ran down the river
'Twas like it was an Italian gondola
When the gondola went rushing past
'Twas like it was making the froth from brushing your teeth.

Rebecca Pearson (10)
Holmlea Primary School

IF

If my mum was a pot of paint
She would be a bright yellow like the shining sun
Beaming cheerfulness everywhere.

If my mum was a bird
She would be a proud peacock
Wearing brightly coloured clothes.

If my mum was an animal
She would be a lovely white Persian cat
Walking proudly in the bright green grass.

If my mum was a flower
She would be a bright pink rose
Shining in the summer sun making everyone feel happy.

Emma Malcolm (9)
Holmlea Primary School

THE STORM

It was raging with anger
must have been upset
mad and dangerous it was
twirling, twisting, turning
blowing the fences away
scary, frightening
all these horrible things
big and bigger it grew
I don't know why it was mad
hurricane, tornado
I really don't know
what it was.

George Spence (10)
Kildrum Primary School

THE STORM

Here we are looking out to sea,
looking for a fair wind heading our way,
the air it looks fine, the sea as well.
Here we go, we set out to sea,
the air still fine and so are we.
Everything is fine until . . .
the wind gets heavier,
a storm is gathering,
we are really getting scared now.
We're running, screaming, shouting and shaking,
we don't know what to do.
We're running and screaming,
we're everywhere.
The rain is falling as hard as hail,
we're swaying side to side,
we nearly tipped over but the wind kept us up.
The skies are full of anger,
the sea is very bumpy and we are cold and scared
and then up came the biggest wave we've ever seen.
I couldn't believe my eyes at first,
but I knew I had to believe that we are all going to die!
Then I saw a rubbing ring,
the wave just hit us and we tipped right over,
but just before I hit the water
I jumped off the ship and swam to the ring.
I watched the ship sink
and after a while the ship was a wreck,
I was lucky to have survived.

Karina McLeod (10)
Kildrum Primary School

TO A TURTLE

Aye, I saw a turtle, 'twas a leather-back
It moved so cautiously, so slow.
A little bit of speed that is what he did lack
And I hope he didn't have far to go.

Aye, I saw a turtle, 'twas a blueish, greenish-red
It had all the colours of the rainbow.
A little bit of fish, that it was fed
And a wee bit of cod roe.

Aye, I saw a turtle, 'twas a nice little fellow
For him the sun always shone.
In his eyes he looked rather mellow
Because he knew he had to get goin'.

Aye, I saw a turtle, 'twas a gory sight
It had blood marks all over his neck.
Had it been attacked in the darkness of night?
Maybe the gulls had had a wee peck.

Graham Whitton (10)
Kildrum Primary School

SNAPSHOT

Adele holding Aarron
Standing so happy
Aarron wriggling
The priest saying a prayer to God
I miss Adele even more now
She's gone with Tony
I still have her in my mind
She's gone up and up and up.

Spike Campbell (11)
Kildrum Primary School

THE STORM

The storm is coming
Everybody hide
Crackling, swirling, banging and bumping,
There's a very high tide.

The banging, the bumping,
The roar of the wind,
Shaking little children, shouting,
Bad, bad wind.

The twister, the wind,
The screeching, the blowing sands,
The rumbling noises,
We feel the icicles hanging from our hands.

The rain has stopped,
The storm has past,
The houses are ruined,
Everyone is fixing them very, very fast.

Laura Grant (10)
Kildrum Primary School

SNAPSHOT

Me and my grandma
happy
two years ago in May
in her house in the kitchen
talking to me, making my breakfast
the kitchen and the window
happy, grateful, joyful
her red dressing gown and slippers.

Andrew Fyffe (10)
Kildrum Primary School

THE TURTLE

A lovely creature with powerful flippers
that waft in the sea and its hard, hard shell,
we think it's a house on the turtle's back
but to a turtle it could be quiet different.
Its shell could be heavy, its shell could be light
in the fresh air, on land, its shell can be dull
but in the sea its shell is so bright.
Its jaws are so strong and its eyes so small
blinking so slowly, it swims so steadily
and that's the turtle, a lovely creature.

Marcus Angiolini (10)
Kildrum Primary School

STORM

Crackle, bang!
Oh no a storm is here,
The rain, the noise, it's terrible.
Crackle, bang!
Thunder, lightning,
Droplets splashing down,
Crackle, bang!
Waves crashing,
Flooding is coming.
Crackle, bang!
Lightning like a pitch fork
Darting through the sky.
I feel like I could *die!*

Misha Connell (10)
Kildrum Primary School

THE STORM

The rainclouds gathered and lightning struck
this is the night of the underworld
the rain hammered down on our home
waves crashed into our farms
nobody thinks anything will survive
this is my nightmare
raindrops fall and children scream
this is the worst night of my life
I cannot help but to think of Billy
where are you my brother?
But what is this
a glimmer of hope
sun!

Scott Tominey (10)
Kildrum Primary School

THE TURTLE

He glides through the water with ease
The massive turtle wistfully sweeps through the
                              underwater world
His eyes so soft
His face so wrinkled
His gentle smile so soft and reassuring
A massive shell is his home
And slides in when in danger
His shell so colourful
And his head and flippers push out from caves
This creature is wonderful in every way.

Claire Laura Semple (10)
Kildrum Primary School

THE TURTLE

Once I found a turtle stranded on a beach
I wanted to see if he could get to the ocean
He tried and he tried and he tried
But he couldn't quite reach
I thought I would give him some food
I tried mosquitoes and shrimps
But I guess he wasn't in the mood
After a while I gave him a pull
Then I fell on his shell
Which felt quite cool
Then I thought I would give him a drink
And then he headed for the sea
After a couple of minutes his shell began to sink
I knew now it was time to say goodbye
But when I walked away
I felt a tear in my eye.

David Easton (10)
Kildrum Primary School

THE STORM

The storm is big and angry,
The wind is outside,
Raindrops falling all around us,
The thunder and lightning is out there, I know.
The tide is getting higher and higher,
The wind is getting stronger and stronger.
I feel all alone, no one with me,
I can see a black cloud coming.
Is it a hurricane?
Is it a tornado?
Will the rain ever stop?

Lisa Devine (10)
Kildrum Primary School

THE TURTLE

His big, hard shell, his home on his back,
as long as a bed and wider.
His face is like a two hundred year old man,
wizened and wrinkled and wise.
His gently, smiling mouth, his little beady eyes,
his home's in the sea, not on the land.
As he swims peacefully in the sea,
just cruising out through the turquoise water,
going further and further out to sea.
His flippers move slowly as he swims.
He's lived a hundred years, seeing many wonderful things.
He's the gentleman of the sea, how long's he got to live?
His shell is like a rainbow gleaming in the sun.
He's seen so many things in his life,
but this adventure's only just begun.

Marina Elizabeth Hunter Phillips (10)
Kildrum Primary School

SNAPSHOT

My dad and I
two years ago,
sitting in the garden
cuddling me,
there were flowers,
a very nice man,
Donald,
black hair,
happy.

Sheona Cullen (10)
Kildrum Primary School

ALONE

All alone in the house, I feel sad,
won't someone please help.
Inside I feel tingly but I'm jumping for joy,
I can't hear a sound, not even my dad,
the noisiest person on Earth.
I sit with my teddy, I cuddle him tight,
I walk down the hall to see where the
slight chime is coming from.
But everything's still, nothing is moving,
as if time has just stopped.
The air is surrounding my silent thoughts
that's if I have any.
I feel a presence is near,
I don't dare to breathe, then eventually
I can't hold it any longer, I gasp for a breath.
The house is not silent now, everyone's up,
so I now think it's time that I should
shut up.

Aileen Alicia Wyatt (10)
Kildrum Primary School

BACK IN THE DEEP BLUE SEA

Today I washed up on the bay,
Unlikely to get back in to the sea,
Rotting away bit by bit every day.
Today a young lad came to help me,
Later I left the bay, he was sad.
Even I was sad, but I'm back in the deep blue sea.

Matthew Love (10)
Kildrum Primary School

THE TURTLE

Down on a beach
You would see lots
Of wonderful sea creatures

But have you ever
Come across
A big, massive, long
Old turtle?

He has a face
Like a two hundred
Year old man.

Wizened and wrinkled
And wise with a gentle
Smiling mouth.

Well, if you do
Come across
The turtle
Always remember
He likes
Blue jellyfish!

Emma Sadler (10)
Kildrum Primary School

THE STORM

S   is for storm, a big chaos creator
T   is for tears of rain falling from the sky
O   is for orchids being battered by the wind and rain
R   is for ruins, as most buildings are
M   is for mortar used to repair houses with bricks.

James William Dewar (10)
Kildrum Primary School

SNAPSHOT

My grandad
three years ago in a nice garden
really nice big smile
hugging my gran
nice shade of blue sky
sun as bright as a lamp
happy!

Danielle Gilmour (10)
Kildrum Primary School

SNAPSHOT

My dad at the beach
two years ago, sitting
in the sand looking
about, people, sand, water,
boats, seaweed and rocks
I love and treasure this
picture forever and ever
and ever.

Jamie Pearson (10)
Kildrum Primary School

SNAPSHOT

Me and my cousin
The seaside
Sandcastles on the sand
Two months ago
We ran into the freezing water
We didn't know we had a picture taken.

Dionne Tominey (10)
Kildrum Primary School

SNAPSHOT

Uncle Chuck last year
sitting in his MG sports car
drinking his tea
trees rustling
cars flying past behind him
happy uncle Chuck.

Euan Russell (10)
Kildrum Primary School

ABANDONED BY THE STORM

A is for most of gone already
B is for bon voyage to our island
A is for our family going away
N is for the noise and panic
D is for home, deserted
O is for the ocean, which is like a pack of wolves
N is for our neighbours, who might to make it
E is for everyone on the mainland
D is for the way I feel as I could die.

Caroline Blair Wheeler Williams (10)
Kildrum Primary School

MYSELF

My knees are steel helmets for battling for the ball
My eyes are like squishy balloons always floating about
My ears are phones made for listening
My hair is threads of wool to keep my head warm
My feet are nice and smelly which attracts all the quality shoes.

Barry Douglas (11)
Mosspark Primary School

My Uncle

If my uncle was an ice cream
he would be mint chocolate chip
because he is full of taste and full of surprises,
He would be cold and taste good.
If my uncle was a cartoon
he would be Homer Simpson
because he is greedy, lazy
and very funny,
he would be a couch potato.
If my uncle was music
he would be rock music
because he is loud and
you can hear him in a crowd,
he would be outrageous.

Catherine Collins (11)
Mosspark Primary School

One To Ten

One wicked witch went to a wedding
Two terrible teachers talked about tennis
Three tough tigers went to the theatre
Four florists sold fake flowers for fun
Five flammable fireworks set fire to the floor
Six sewage snakes shampooed themselves
Seven service stations shrank to shreds
Eight alligators joined the army to act
Nine naughty geese never had neighbours
Ten toads lost their tongues.

Fraser McIntyre (10)
Mosspark Primary School

MY EYES

My eyes are blue flecked with yellow and white.
As yellow as a sunny morning,
sparkling in your windows.
As yellow as a duck's beak,
fishing for his dinner.
As white as a shining moon,
floating in the sky.
As white as a dove's feathers,
flying really high.
As blue as a sparkling waterfall,
tumbling high.
As blue as a dolphin,
jumping for joy.

Craig MacDonald (9)
Mosspark Primary School

MY EYES

My eyes are rich brown,
as brown as chocolate
melting in my mouth.
As brown as a hedgehog,
curling into a ball.
As brown as a conker,
lying in the garden.
As brown as sweet coffee,
rich and hot.
As brown as a rich cake,
with cherry topping.
As brown as a tree trunk,
all bare without its leaves.

Shafaq Khan (9)
Mosspark Primary School

CHAIN OF THOUGHTS

Cosy winter's night
Christmas tree is glowing bright
Shining like a star

Stars hang in the sky
Nearly falling down to Earth
But still hang till day

The light autumn day
Leaves tumbling through the branches
Then travelling on.

The tree stands proudly
Letting children play on it
Without complaining.

Watching children play
Splashing in all the puddles
Getting soaking wet.

Splashing in the sea
On holiday at the beach
Stay here all day long.

The shivering day
Drags on, another day ends
Christmas gets nearer.

Ashley Prior (10)
Mosspark Primary School

MY MUM

If my mum were a flower
she would be a rose
smelling lovely with her thorns
she would stand tall and straight.

If my mum were a drink
she would be champagne
she would stand in the glass and
move and dance with joy
she is lively and bubbly.

If my mum were an animal
she would be a tigress
she would be standing her ground
caring for her cubs.

If my mum were a cartoon
she would be Tweetie Pie
she is sweet with a cute face
but sharp with her eye.

Holly McDonald (11)
Mosspark Primary School

GOODBYE!

Oh, must you go
I won't stand it
but if you die
I will cry and mourn forever and ever
so this is goodbye

Oh, please be careful
I will wait at the train station until your train goes
so this is goodbye

I'll give you my handkerchief to remember me by
so this is goodbye

Oh, I'll be so sad and miserable
and I will be alone with my family
but I'll try to be brave
so this is goodbye!

Diane Dick (11)
Mosspark Primary School

MY SISTER

If my sister was a flower
she would be a rose
because she's beautiful and brightens up the day
she stands tall and strong all day long.

If my sister was a drink
she would be apple juice
because she is sweet and full of surprises
freshly squeezed she is.

If my sister was an animal
she would be a fox
because she is sly and cunning
and roams about the forest.

If my sister was a colour
she would be yellow
because she is bright and cheery like the sun
shines bright in rain or shine.

Amanda Gow (11)
Mosspark Primary School

MY DAD

If my dad was a drink
he would be a cocktail
because he has lots of layers
and is full of surprises.

If my dad was a kind of music
he would be rock
because he is loud and popular
and lots of people listen to him.

If my dad was a bird
he would be an eagle
because he is fast and brave
and people look up to him.

If my dad was an animal
he would be a lion
because he is strong and fierce
and people are scared of him.

Ross MacDonald (11)
Mosspark Primary School

TITANIC POEM!

Shiny funnels painted black and white,
Fast engines just going to be used,
Expensive steel made the ship.

People waving goodbye to families,
Waves splashing against the ship,
Excited children going to New York.

The dark cold sea comes roaring in,
Parents are screaming for help,
Children crying, they don't want to die.

Broken instruments that belonged to the band,
A creepy feeling because of the darkness,
Children's toys all covered in rust.

Laura-Marie Gormley (9)
Mosspark Primary School

MY LITTLE SISTER

If my sister was a colour
she would be orange
full of energy
happy and cheery.

If my sister was a flower
she would be a poppy
loving and caring
always bright and sparkling.

If my sister was a fruit
she would be a mango
she is exotic
always wanting an adventure.

If my sister was an animal
she would be a fluffy kitten
she's lovely and cuddly
playful and cute!

Amy Pollok (11)
Mosspark Primary School

RENGA

Snowy afternoon
And the wind is blowing wild
Like the winter's breath

The breath of the dead
Lies still through the night cool air
We remember them

I can remember
When you were a little boy
You used to like sweets

Sweets are sugary
They only cost ten pennies
You liked them so much

You were a good boy
You are healthy and child-like
Now you're all grown up

I can hear the rain
It is tumbling like a rock
All I want is peace

Peace is very quiet
It only comes in winter
In a snowy night

Snowy afternoon
And the wind is blowing wild
Like the winter's breath.

Iain Slorance (10)
Mosspark Primary School

CHAIN OF THOUGHTS

Frosty winter's morn
Frozen breath comes out my mouth
Like wind blowing trees

Trees reach for the sky
Cotton clouds tickle its branches
As it grasps the sun

Cloudy nights so cold
Stars are watching over us
Angels kiss our eyes

Lamps light up the house
Even in the day it's dark
Light a warm candle

Flame from candle
Only thing keeping me hot
A cup of warm tea

Cream on my pudding
Like snow lying on the ground
Snowman standing tall

Snowman dressed up warm
Fairy lights and Christmas trees
Winter's back again.

Jacqueline Lindsay (10)
Mosspark Primary School

AUTUMN RENGA

Cold autumn evening
The fire crackling bright
Like the sun shining

A house on fire
Until the ruin stands black
House burnt out and black

Red and green apples
Hang on the old apple tree
Waiting to be picked

Trees sway in the wind
Windy night in November
Branches crashing down

Birds tossed by the wind
Sparrows chirping in the trees
The newborn birds cry

Planes at an airport
Getting ready to take off
Other planes come down

Like autumn leaves fall
Floating down through misty air
Sparkling frosty leaves.

Christopher McCabe (10)
Mosspark Primary School

RENGA

Sunny summer morn
Birds tweet happily on twigs
A choir singing

Choir sings softly
People love their joyful songs
They stand and listen

They stand for the bus
The bus that always comes late
To go to the shops

Shopping with my friends
We go for our breakfast
Our food is good

It smells of roses
Some people pick these
Life for them is short

A good life I have
Freedom some don't have today
Like the slaves that work

They sing when they work
Singing songs about freedom
In the sunny land.

Gemma Coulston (9)
Mosspark Primary School

Renga

Cosy winter night
Children playing their PlayStation
Like frozen statues

Statues in the park
Standing tall with birds on them
High above they watch

Vultures flying high
Swooping down low, eating prey
Taking away a life

The life of a bird
Small and afraid it cries of fear
A small animal

A silent tiger
Chasing its terrified, scared prey
Chasing its breakfast

Delicious breakfast
His mouth is watering, but
Can he catch his food?

Hard in the winter
There's no more left here now
Just children playing.

John Hugh Connor (10)
Mosspark Primary School

CHAIN OF THOUGHTS

Cold frosty evening
making people cold and dull
like a Viking raid.

Vikings get ready
for a raid in Lindisfarne
coming in the ships.

The ships skim the sea
turquoise sea and golden sands
for us to enjoy.

Enjoy holidays
jumping in the crystal pool
eating ice-lollies.

Sunshine, sand and fun
relax and bathe in the sun
playing in the pool.

Splashing through the waves
fresh, cool water in the sea
jumping in and out.

Jumping in the leaves
around the frozen puddles
having fun in winter.

Jade Stewart (10)
Mosspark Primary School

CHAIN OF THOUGHTS

Breezy autumn night,
Golden and brown leaves falling,
Like birds flying down.

Birds diving for fish,
Orange and blue under the sea,
Where they like to swim.

Dogs swimming like frogs,
Smoothly and with a rhythm,
Then they come to shore.

Nice sandy seashore,
Swim in the sea with my friends,
For a cool day out.

Cool ice-lollies melt,
Cola making us thirsty,
Now let's eat burgers.

Burgers in the pan,
Sparks are flying everywhere,
Like a fire starting.

Barbecues flaring,
The leaping flames are golden,
Like leaves falling down.

Nicola Munro (10)
Mosspark Primary School

CHAIN OF THOUGHTS

Breezy winter's night,
Grasses dance in the moonlight,
Like girls at discos.

Loud music blaring,
Shouting against the music,
Laughter - excitement.

Crying with laughter,
Men joking with each other,
While walking down the streets.

Streets cold and windy,
People wrapped up warmly,
Shiver in the cold.

Warm and welcome home,
Sleeping tight in your bed,
Watching your dreams.

Dreams of gentle joy,
Watching the moonlight dancers,
Fly in the sky.

Breezy night, sleep tight,
Grasses swaying to and fro,
Songs go on and on.

Mairi Campbell (10)
Mosspark Primary School

A RENGA CHAIN

Hot summer's evening,
Sun is setting in the sky,
Like a sinking ship.

Water pulling down,
Everything it sees in sight,
Drowning in its water.

Water steaming blood,
War ships are nowhere to be seen,
But today they come.

The sun is glowing,
The boats are sailing across,
The sea glows light blue.

The summer goes on,
People living happily,
Joyfully with glee.

The oceans re clear,
No more ships bringing black death,
Now the summer stays.

Summer days are back,
Gulls are coming to seashore
Like a memory.

Marc MacCallum (10)
Mosspark Primary School

RENGA

Cold autumn morning
Robins chirping happily
Like stringed harps playing.

The orchestra plays -
Trumpets, violins and drums
Play a Christmas tune.

Santa wraps up warm
Then goes out to feed his deer
Sits at the fire.

Fire burning chopped wood
Crackling heat, comfort and warmth
Tired people sleep.

Mum turning in bed
Dreaming where money comes from
Does it grow on trees?

Christmas is so near
It brings presents - and worries
Oh Christmas is near.

Winter is coming
Santa climbs down the chimney
Autumn is gone now.

Jennifer Hutton (10)
Mosspark Primary School

CHAIN OF THOUGHT

A hot summer day
Children rolling in the sand
A band of angels.

A child climbing ropes
Like a cat that chases mice
For food and for fun.

People chase weak people
As something has terrorised them
As they are happy.

Hungry children eat
In a land where famine lives
So they are fearful.

Here the joy of snow
Sparkling like a king's treasure
But not for that child.

Dying like the trees
Birds leave the cold winter
Flying to the sun.

Angels with white wings
Soft clouds in the blue summer sky
Smile on the children.

Greg Quinn (10)
Mosspark Primary School

AUTUMN

A bundant leaves scattered around, mellow colours, yellow
and brown
U nder the maple tree you will find kids kicking leaves
T awny leaves on the trees, falling off and down like bees
U ntil spring no leaves on trees, autumn brushes them off
M any little shivers and we know autumn's here and Christmas
is near
N ovember night in your house, say goodbye to autumn.

Paul Milne (10)
Mosspark Primary School

MY EYES

My eyes are greyish blue,

As grey as a pigeon,
Resting on his nest.

As grey as fresh dew,
Falling onto grass.

As grey as winter air,
Chilly - but exciting.

As blue as a summer sky,
Warm weather and fun.

As blue as the ocean deep,
With fishes of all kinds.

As blue as an Eskimo,
Cosy in his igloo.

Claire Dyer (9)
Mosspark Primary School

WHO DO YOU THINK YOU ARE?

Who do you think you are,
Scribbling over my homework,
Messing up my room,
Flushing my head down the toilet?

Who do you think you are,
Painting on my uniform,
Putting slugs in my dinner,
Putting clowns in my room?

Who do you think you are,
Throwing me out the window,
Stealing my teacher's bag,
Cutting the grass with my teeth?

Just who do you think you are?

Sara MacCallum (9)
Mosspark Primary School

THE SEA

The sea is a super speed panther,
He looks so strong and powerful,
He rolls on the beach all day with his giant legs and arms
And when the night wind roars
And the moon rocks in the stormy cloud,
He hunts very fast and pounces so high,
But on quiet days of May or June when even the grasses on the dune
Play no more their reedy tune,
He goes to sleep for his rest,
So quiet, so quiet he can scarcely be heard.

Grant McKigen (9)
Mosspark Primary School

THE SEA

The sea is an angry polar bear,
Strong and rough,
He runs about mad looking for fish all day,
With his strong rough paws and sharp teeth in his jaws,
Hour upon hour he looks for fish for dinner,
The rumbling tumbling stones, he kicks them with his feet,
And when the night wind roars,
And the moon rocks in the stormy cloud,
He will run about mad and make footprints in the sandy dunes,
But on quiet days of May or June,
When even the grasses on the dune play no more their reedy tune,
With his large thick fat body,
He lies down, then yawns and snores so quiet,
So quiet, he scarcely can be heard.

Keira McLellan (9)
Mosspark Primary School

THE SEA

The sea is a fat polar bear
He looks enormous and big
He walks slowly
With his large claws and paws
And when the night wind roars
And the moon rocks in the stormy cloud
He jumps quickly into his cave to escape
But on quiet days of May or June
When even the grasses on the dune
Play no more their reedy tune
He curls into a big ball fast asleep.

Amy McLellan (9)
Mosspark Primary School

MYSELF

My hands are claws
for grabbing things.
My eyes are pool balls
for potting with.
My head is a football
for scoring into the back of the net.
My nose is a chicken nugget
smelling delicious.
My fingers are strains of wheat
for holding seeds.
My ears are doors
for gossip to go into.
My teeth are jugs
for milk to go into.
My legs are branches
for kids to swing on.
My blood is a river
going to a red ocean.
My mouth is a black hole
for things to disappear into.

Steven Barrowman (11)
Mosspark Primary School

MY MUM

If my mum was an animal
she would be a tiger
clever and never scared.

If my mum was a circus act
she would be a clown
funny, wacky and always having a good time.

If my mum was a country
she would be America
organised, neat and never out of money.

Ross Carstairs (11)
Mosspark Primary School

A GIFT FOR A CHILD

To make you strong,
I bring you hair from a horse
From the farm in Spain.

To make you a hunter,
I bring you a smooth falcon's feather
From the ice caves in Russia.

To make you a farmer,
I bring you a golden seed
From the farm in England.

To make you a thief,
I bring you a gold coin
From the monasteries of Iona.

To make you a sailor,
I bring you a curved wooden boat
From Lindisfarne.

To make you powerful,
I bring you a horn of a bull
From the forests of Germany.

Pray Odin you grow to be a great Viking.

Chirelle Fitzpatrick (9)
Mosspark Primary School

LIES

This morning on my way to school,
seventy nine warriors tried to kill me!

The colour yellow blinded me
and I had to go the doctor's.

Little Miss Muffet tried to pour
hot porridge all over me.

A mad driver tried to knock me down
and then he drove off a cliff.

A tiger was eating my dog and then
it broke his tooth and swallowed it.

There was a tornado and it almost captured me.
I was so happy I made it, I almost had a heart attack.

A huge dinosaur came into my house
and ate my homework and my dinner!

Sorry I'm late, Miss!

Stephanie Gormley (11)
Mosspark Primary School

MY EYES!

My eyes are browny black with flecks of amber,
As brown as the crust of new-baked bread,
As brown as a shining conker, hiding in the autumn leaves,
As amber as the autumn leaves falling from the trees,
As amber as the sun, on a summer's evening,
As black as a settled night, waiting for a bit of light,
As black as a shadow on the sun.

Robert Orr (9)
Mosspark Primary School

THE SEA

The sea is a frightening lion,
Moving sharply and shaggily,
He darts on the sand all day,
With is white sharp teeth and brown eyes,
Hour upon hour he eats his prey,
The rumbling tumbling stones,
Licking his hairy paws,
And when the night wind roars,
And the moon rocks in the stormy cloud,
He darts and leaps in the dark sky,
But on quiet days of May or June,
When even the grasses on the dune,
Play no more their reedy tune,
With his face in between his paws,
He lies down and falls asleep.

Hayley Weinman (9)
Mosspark Primary School

MY GRANDAD

If my grandad was a bird he would be an
owl as he is the wisest in the family.

If he was a colour he would be dark blue
like the night sky with the stars shining
bright, watching over me at night.

If he was food he'd be pasta, nice and soft
covered in mild sauce.

If he was a flower he'd be a thistle standing
proud in Scotland shouting for freedom.

Michaela Muir (11)
Mosspark Primary School

LIES!

This morning on my way to school,
Eighty dogs bigger than houses chased me down the street.
This morning on my way to school,
Black and blue punched me.
This morning on my way to school,
Little Miss Muffet rolled down hills with me!
This morning on my way to school,
I got rolled around on bus wheels for an hour.
This morning on my way to school,
A rhinoceros chased me through the jungle.
This morning on my way to school,
A twister chased me and took me for a ride on the wild side.

Because all of these exciting and fun things happened,
I was late for school.

Kirsty Aitcheson (11)
Mosspark Primary School

FOOTBALL BOOTS

My new football boots,
I like them a lot.
They are red and black ones,
So I can take a powerful shot.
The ball went past the keeper
And right into the goal.
When it hit the football net,
It almost made a hole.

Ross Hocknull (11)
Mosspark Primary School

MY MUM

If my mum was a flower
she would be a rose
because she smells nice and
brightens up my day when I see her.

If my mum was a piece of music
she would be pop music
because she likes to jump and
dance to it.

If my mum was a colour
she would be pink
because she is always
soft and gentle.

If my mum was a drink
she would be milk
because she is strong
and healthy.

Angela McManus (11)
Mosspark Primary School

AUTUMN

A bundant supply of leaves scattered all over the ground
U ntidy leaves in the paths of driveways
T rees are nearly bare as the wind blows the leaves off
U nwinding leaves on the roads
M isty hills like a ghost covering it
N uts that squirrels gather before winter comes in.

Omar Azam (11)
Mosspark Primary School

MYSELF

My fingers are piano keys
for playing a song.
My lashes are strands of grass
swaying in the grass.
My neck is a tree trunk
growing from my shoulders.
My hair is strands of wheat
gathered for harvest.
My nose is a small hill
growing step by step all the way to the top.
My eyebrows are rabbits
jumping through the long lush grass.
My arms are branches
sticking out from a tree.
My feet are flippers
cutting through the sea.
My legs are curtain rails
long and thin.
My mouth is a cave
going on for ever and ever.

Hayley Smith (11)
Mosspark Primary School

AUTUMN

A mber coloured leaves falling off the trees, dancing in the breeze
U nder all these beautiful leaves lie some honey bees
T wisting, twirling, all around the leaves fall down
U nruly children all around playing in the leaves
M isty moon in the sky, leaves go flying by
N ovember after autumn, snow falls.

Alan McGarrity (11)
Mosspark Primary School

I AM NOT AMUSED

I am not amused
Boring children everywhere
Telling jokes but I don't care
Sitting down watching TV
Everyone laughs but me.
School is cool but language is boring,
In wet plays I watch rain pouring.
Drip. Drop,
Like a tap with no stop.
Making shapes with my food,
All I can say is, 'I am not amused.
Tidying up the whole house,
I drop off to sleep without a peep.
Listening to talking and throwing balls.
Dreaming of a music and dancing hall.
Everything 'they' do,
I am not amused.

Lewa Thomas (11)
Notre Dame Primary School

HOMEWORK

Homework, homework is so boring,
I need to do homework in the morning.
Homework, homework is so hard
Homework, homework makes me mad.
Homework, homework takes so long,
I feel like singing songs.
Homework, homework is not
better than any other work.

Nabila Arshad (11)
Notre Dame Primary School

THE GRANNY ON THE TOP FLOOR

The granny on the top floor,
She's always out giving chores,
Wash the doors,
Clean the street
And when you come in,
Wipe your feet.

Jean's daughter, Maggie, went up and said,
'Why don't *you* do it
Or do you lie in your bed?'

Old baths and sinks,
They lie in our street
And make it stink,
It's like wearing socks over four years,
Without being washed.

If you can't help we'll have to dodge
The granny on the top floor,
Help! Help!
She's gave us 20 chores.

Ah! Ah! My hands are sore.

Claire Reilly (11)
Notre Dame Primary School

WORLD WAR II

The room is silent and dark,
but outside there are bombs dropping onto buildings.
The radio is still on low,
I just feel like screaming,
but I can't make a noise.

The room is cold, damp and small,
my bones feel all funny like jelly.
Everyone is sitting still, not making a noise.
Everything is still and everyone is quiet.
I just feel like screaming,
but I can't make a noise.

Sarah Graham (11)
Notre Dame Primary School

RUARIDH

I have a brother called Ruaridh
He drives me up the wall
He used to dress up as a girl
And play with Barbie dolls
He'll kill me for writing this poem
But I don't give a toss
I just won't let him read this
It'll be his loss
He won't give me any peace
When I'm trying to do some work
Wherever I look, he'll be there
Round the corner he'll lurk
It's amazing how annoying
The little brat can be
Every hour of every day
He's the biggest pain you'll see
He's annoying in everything he does
Even when he gets up for a drink

But he can be quite nice sometimes
I love him really, I think.

Laura May Frize (11)
Notre Dame Primary School

My Morning

I wake up in the morning
and get changed into my uniform.
I have breakfast and watch telly.
I get ready to leave
with my jacket on
and my bag on my shoulder.
Every day outside it gets colder.
I walk to the bus stop
to get the bus.
When I do, I go up to the top.
I get dropped off and walk to school.
This is my morning.

Colm McGuire (11)
Notre Dame Primary School

Dragons

Dragons fierce, green creatures.
Scales and winged creatures.
Fire-breathing and yellow-eyed creatures.
Lives in cold, wet, spooky caves,
Kidnaps young, beautiful maids.
Fights handsome knights on white horses,
Steals farmers' animals for food.

A myth creature
Dragon!

Victoria Culshaw (11)
Notre Dame Primary School

WHAT ARE THOSE THINGS?

What are those things
They teach in class?
Are they robots like C-3PO,
Or are they real like you and me?
Do they come from Kelvindale
Or is it space like Mighty Mouse?
Are they Martians
Or are they animals?
Tell me go on!
What are those things?

Kirsty Douglas (10)
Notre Dame Primary School

MY FRIEND THE SEAGULL

My friend is like a seagull
He flaps around all day
He flies away when it gets through
And comes back next day
He's never really lazy
He's always on the job
He's best for keeping secrets
He never brings it up
That's why Colm is the friend for me.

Stuart Armit (11)
Notre Dame Primary School

I Still Remember

It happened 8 years ago
I still remember the feeling
The room went cold
I couldn't wait any longer
I heard a scream
What was wrong?
I barged in
A tender baby's cry . . .
I'm a sister!

Rebecca Fergus (10)
Ravenswood Primary School

Dinner Time

When Mum shouts out, 'It's dinner time.'
And under a second we're ready to eat
My mum throws out the slushed eyeballs
Delight!
We stuff it down like pigs in the mud
That's what it's like when my mum shouts
'Dinner time!'

Paul Coulter (10)
Ravenswood Primary School

The Eclipse

Two worlds collide,
Two places side by side.
As two worlds collide,
Two planets subside.

Two lights align,
Two aliens attack.
Two astronauts die,
Two worlds destroyed.

Andrew Carmichael (10)
Ravenswood Primary School

HORRID SPIDERS

Horrid spiders creeping on my bed,
Some of the spiders sleep on my head.
I wake up in the middle of the night,
I jump from my bed and throw on the light.
Just as I thought,
It was all a dream.
I was so frightened,
I just had to scream.

Rebecca Main (10)
Ravenswood Primary School

BIRTHDAY

B ring yourself along after all
I t's my birthday, don't forget to call
R emember to bring some party things
T he apple pies so crunchy
H appy days are here again for it's my birthday
D on't forget to bring your appetite
A fer all there'll be so much to eat
Y ou'll never eat any dinner.

Cairn MacFarlane (10)
Ravenswood Primary School

CHRISTMAS

C hristmas bells everywhere
H olly dangling on the snow-covered doors
R obins hunting for food in the thick snow
I cicles hanging from the white rooftops
S nowmen standing in the ice cold air
T offee dripping off the tall, round cake
M erry people singing like an orchestra
A special tree decorated with Christmas jewels
S nowflakes fall from the dark night sky.

Ross McLachlan (10)
Ravenswood Primary School

ME AND MY FRIEND

Me and my friend bonded like
nothing on Earth.
She filled my world with happiness.
We did everything together.
But one day,
She was torn away.
My life crumbled . . .
And even now I can see her
Smiling at me.

Joanna Cameron (10)
Ravenswood Primary School

GOODBYE

Goodbye to you forever more
Goodbye to the grease all over the floor
Goodbye to the leaking pipes so fat
Even the mouldy carpets and front doormat

Goodbye to the view that was so grey
Now it's green as bright as day
Goodbye to the house that I adore
Goodbye to my house forever more.

Holly Scotland (10)
Ravenswood Primary School

BON VOYAGE!

Bon voyage to that shop (and that building)
I'll miss you very much
For all the presents you gave me
And all the kindness and love you surrounded me with.
I've got a tear in my eye.
I'm stepping onto the plane.
Bon voyage *Las Vegas!*

Lynn Baillie (10)
Ravenswood Primary School

CHRISTMAS TIME

C hitter-chatter, I am ever so cold, I am like a snowball
H elp, I need a doctor I'm freezing
R udolf with a nose so cold
I f I go out, every icicle attaches to me in every way
S chool days are gone for many weeks *freedom*
T he trees all sparkle with gleaming joy
M agnificent turkeys make houses as hot as a Jacuzzi
A ll the streets are as white as Heaven
S mack, I am in bed, goodbye.

Daryn Murphy (10)
Ravenswood Primary School

THE SWEET WAVES

The sweet waves
splash over the yawning stars.
The lighthouse hears nothing
but the cries of the waves.
The sweet waves
cover the rocks and
they breathe no more.

The sweet waves
cover the decks of
the dying sailors
and diving
they're not surviving
and breathe their
last breath.

The sweet waves
cover the land
and someone somewhere
is dying and dying
and there's no one there to rescue.

The sweet waves
end, end, end
die, die, die
until they fade away
and are no more.

Alistair Yule (9)
Ravenswood Primary School

MY WORST DAY EVER

My clothes were totally dirty
My bag had snapped in half
My hair was tangled in knots
And my face was full of spots.

Then I ordered the taxi at ten o'clock
But it came at ten past ten
He drove at five miles per hour
With springs popping out of the seats
I never thought I would say this
Hurry up and get me to school.

Sarah Brynes (10)
Ravenswood Primary School

HALLOWE'EN

H ollow winds rush through the woods,
A ll the trees sway and groan.
L ost in the woods without a torch
L ocked inside with people out.
O nly you are amongst the trees,
W ishing you were in your bed.
E' very day, every night,
E eeeak! Why tonight?
N ever leave the house on Hallowe'en!

Meltem Kesal (10)
Ravenswood Primary School

PIRATES

P irates are evil
I n their little boat
R ound and fat, they are ugly, like an old, old goat
A t night they have a feast
T ill morning they look like a couple of beasts
E mpty food tins and empty beer bottles, never clean up
S o then they all died from sharks that came and ate them all up.

Katrina Woods (10)
Rogerfield Primary School

PIRATES

P irates sail on the sea
I n the sea there are lots of different things
R oger is a bad pirate
A rchie has only one leg
T reasures are very good
E very pirate can be bad
S ome pirates have patches over their eyes.

Sarah Baillie (10)
Rogerfield Primary School

PIRATES

P irates sail ships
I n the sea pirates sometimes find treasure
R eal pirates wear hats
A ll pirates have a flag on their ship
T he pirates are mostly baddies
E very pirate wears an earring
S ome pirates wear patches over their head.

Scott Wilson (10)
Rogerfield Primary School

PLANETS

P luto is the very last planet
L ight is important so it won't be dull
A stronauts are also important too
N ight sky can be lovely with stars
E arth goes round 24 hours a day
T he solar system shows you the planets
S un spot is important because it is the coolest and darkest spot.

Ashleigh Gillies (10)
Rogerfield Primary School

THE PIRATES

P irates are cruel and mean
I 've seen a pirate's ship
R owing to islands I've never seen
A re pirates small or tall?
T here was a pirate named One Eye Jack
E yes? Most of them had only one
S hips are big and crooked.

Jade Grimason (10)
Rogerfield Primary School

PIRATES

P irates are rich because they find gold
I n the sea there is a message in a bottle
R are pirate boats, heavy with gold
A nd every day they go on a search
T he patch on their eye is to cover their socket
E very boat they find they look for treasure
S ometimes the pirates die.

Steven Baillie (10)
Rogerfield Primary School

BOYS, BOYS, I HATE BOYS

I hate boys who huff and puff,
I hate boys who think they're tough,
I hate boys who watch the telly,
Eating ice cream and jelly.
I hate boys who always fight
And laugh at people who've lost their sight!
I hate boys who shrug their shoulders
And always throw some big rough boulders.

Ashley Loughran (11)
Rogerfield Primary School

HOT

I entered a hot room,
There was a soft chair,
I sat on it,
There was a fire,
I could see the sun through
The gaps in the window,
There were bright yellow curtains,
The walls were red,
The carpet was orange
And the ceiling was yellow,
It was so hot, I left.

Karen McFarlane (10)
Rogerfield Primary School

MY HOBBIES

My hobby is drawing,
Yes that is true.
I also like badminton
And basketball too.
And there is line dancing
Oh dear, I can't stop.
I love penny whistle,
I think my head is going to pop.

Kayleigh Baldwin (11)
Rogerfield Primary School

WHAT A JOURNEY TO SPACE!

I am going on a big journey,
to far, far outer space!
But the other spaceship with me . . .
thinks we're having a race!

I am finally up in space,
and I have nothing to fear.
This is my dream place,
as long as I am here.

I like this big place,
no one else here but me.
I'd never want to leave here . . .
all these beautiful sights to see!

I'd never want to leave here,
would I want to? Nope!
I don't know when I'm landing . . .
not too soon, I hope!

Stephen McCann (9)
St Angela's Primary School, Glasgow

SPACE

Space, space, such a wonderful thing
I'd love to land on Saturn's rings.
I'd like to go up to the moon
I hope that I will go there soon.
I'd love to ride the Milky Way
and watch the stars come out to play.
I'd take a trip up to Mars
and then I'd catch a shooting star.
Neptune is the place for me
there are so many things to see.
The hottest star is the sun
if you go there you'll be 'well done'.
Pluto is an amazing place
the last one in the planet race.
Mercury, Venus, Uranus too
I'd love to visit wouldn't you?
But I hope that you will all agree
that Earth is the best place to be.

Halim Boussouara (9)
St Angela's Primary School, Glasgow

SPACE POEM

Space, space, full of planets
orbiting round the sun.
As they loop and coil,
twist and turn.
There's Mercury, Venus, Earth and Mars,
Jupiter, Saturn, Neptune and Pluto.
Neil Armstrong was the first man on the moon . . .
The next one will be up there soon! (Me!)

Liam O'Reilly (9)
St Angela's Primary School, Glasgow

THE ADVENTURE IN SPACE!

I am looking out of my window,
one dark and spooky night.
I see a big moon . . .
shining out at me.
I see the darkness outside,
then I see some shadows,
coming closer and closer!
I hear my heart
pounding, sounding a little scared!
Here comes a space saucer
with aliens, with sparkling smiles.
I walk back and back . . .
'Don't be afraid!
Come on, I'll give you a ride into space!'
So I wasn't afraid after all!

Sabrena Iqbal (9)
St Angela's Primary School, Glasgow

SPACE

I would love to go to space,
maybe I would win a race.
I would love to meet friendly aliens on Mars.
The one thing that I don't like is . . .
the food! They only give you Mars bars!
It would be fun to go on board a
rocket and go up to space.
When I get on the rocket it will go . . .
10, 9, 8, 7, 6, 5, 4, 3, 2, 1, blast-off!
And fly into . . .
Space!

Claire Turner (9)
St Angela's Primary School, Glasgow

MY SPACE POEM

Space, space, in the moon,
when will we be landing?
Soon! 10, 9, 8, 7 . . .
I like Saturn and you like Neptune.
6, 5, 4, 3 . . .
Here we go, I need some tea!
I love space so, so much,
It is great, such a lovely touch!
2, 1, 0 . . . Blast-off!
The rocket is lifting so fast.
Dark night, shining light . . .
Stars twinkle in the night.
Without a sound, as I float away . . .
I see Earth away in the distance.

I thought it was all a dream . . .
as I stepped onto Mars,
I couldn't believe it,
just like a sound of guitars!

Mishka Krause (9)
St Angela's Primary School, Glasgow

THE BLOODY WAR

The war is like a flower
that never grows in the
dark night shade.

The bombs were like fireworks
screaming through the dark night skies
and the going off is just like a lion
roaring in pain.

The guns were so loud
it was like a thousand
nuclear bombs going off.

You can hear soldiers
screaming in pain
in the battlefield as they
fall to their bloody death.

John Murphy (11)
St Angela's Primary School, Glasgow

SPACE

One day I went to my window,
and I said,
'I wish I was on the moon,
in space to have a race,
it would be good.'
I put my T-shirt and my spacesuit on
my moon boots too!
I had my gear and a rocket,
ready to go up to space!
It would be a bit scary!
I'd better go,
before I change my mind!
I'm going to the moon!
I'm ready for adventure . . .
I will be back soon.
With moondust in my pocket,
and pictures in my head,
I'll dream of my adventure,
back in my cosy bed!

Anthony Healy (9)
St Angela's Primary School, Glasgow

FOOTBALL

Walking on the pitch
tall and proud
all of the fans
shouting aloud

Kick off, the time has come
the match has started
it's just begun

Passing here
passing there
call of the players
spread out everywhere

The ball is passed in
to a tall man
he hits the ball
and scored a goal
and the fans shouted
'Offside, it's not a goal.'

Nicky Starnes (11)
St Angela's Primary School, Glasgow

TEACHERS

Teachers are cruel, they think they rule
but really they are just there to teach.
Every teacher thinks they're cool but they just
teach in our school.
All the teachers have to correct our work
and give it out and they always bawl and shout.
Cool they are not, but we are so because children rule!

Helping us in school, the work is often easy,
everyone having a carry on until she screams
because she screams like a firework going off
up in the sky.
Raising their voices to naughty children
signing punishment exercises.

Deborah Layden (11)
St Angela's Primary School, Glasgow

IN A SHUTTLE

Up in the sky the rocket flies
through space,
past Mercury, Venus, Mars and more . . .
through space's
open door.

The flames are burning hot as can be,
soaring and gliding over the sea.

Astronauts floating up and down,
objects and food going round and round.

On the moon they have landed all dirty and sandy,
the astronauts, good and dandy!

Mission completed!
Back to Earth,
travelling again,
this time home to Perth.

Jamie Clark (9)
St Angela's Primary School, Glasgow

ELEMENTS OF EARTH

F lames that rise ever so high
I nto the daylight and night sky
R ipping away lives, you can see fire's power
E veryone knows it could kill the nicest flower.

W avy waves in the sea
A nd water can create
T idal waves that could crush you or me
E lement of water, oh the damage you could do
R ipping apart houses and supermarkets too!

A ir, another element with so much power
I could watch it
R ip away the Eiffel Tower

E arth is an element that keeps its pace
A nd cleverly decides if to keep the human
R ace -
T hough Earth is big and tough, it also deserves 1 big
H ug!

Respect your elements
They are a big fuss
Because with a swipe
Of their hand
They could kill all of us!

James McArdle (11)
St Angela's Primary School, Glasgow

SPACE

Rockets, rockets in the air,
I want to go to space, it's not fair!
I thought and thought and thought and thought,
I were to be an astronaut!
But if I am to change my mind,
I will travel to Mars and find . . .
Rocks and dust, alien rays,
It would be amazing if I could run at an alien pace!
I would fly through hyper space!
Just to win a shuttle race.

Running through Saturn's dust,
Blown away by one big gust!
Flying through the sun's heatwaves,
Stuck in space for days and days.
Getting caught in alien battles,
Noises like giant rattles.
Soon *I'll* be landing on Neptune!
Then I shall visit the moon.
On the moon the rocks are tall,
Compared to them, I'm quite small.
I will dance all night long . . .
And listen to the 'Alien Song'.

Gino Ventre (9)
St Angela's Primary School, Glasgow

THE MOON AND THE SUN

Oh sun, oh sun we need light!
Oh please,
we need light when you are not shining!
Oh the moon! Why oh please sun you have
to shine on the moon.
It will help us on Earth.
The sun was shining at last,
so we were no longer cold.
We live happily now
and with lots of food and water.
We lived safely
in your light!

Sean Bill (9)
St Angela's Primary School, Glasgow

THE MOON

When I look up
out of my window . . .
at the moon
I wonder if there . . .
are aliens on the moon!
If there were,
I'd go up . . .
and make friends with them
and float in space
with them!
I'd go up and see them . . .
every day!

Robert Wynn (9)
St Angela's Primary School, Glasgow

MY DREAM

I dream I go to space
see the moon and stars too . . .
I would put my flag on the moon,
I would like to meet an alien,
ugly and green!
I would ride on his spaceship,
I would collect space rocks.

The alien would show me her family,
there is her mum **"!!*$$**
and her dad !!$&****£! and her sister **%!!"$£
and herself of course!
Spoggy!
Now it's time to say goodbye!
10, 9, 8, 7, 6, 5, 4, 3, 2, 1, 0
Blast-off!

Then I woke up!

Danielle McCabe
St Angela's Primary School, Glasgow

SPACE

'Some day I will go to Mars,' I said
Maybe before I go to bed.
Very adventurous and exciting it would be,
Every day I would see,
More and more stars,
Just in where we are.
Sun will cast light,
Until it is the dark shadowy night.
Nobody knows about it,
Planet and star are it!

Kenny Chu (9)
St Angela's Primary School, Glasgow

A Journey Into Space

Lying down, not such a comfy way,
especially in the spacesuit, very heavy.
Going down with so much pressure,
but not so much leisure.
Here we go . . .
not allowed to change my mind,
going up, leaving the Earth behind!
Looking out the window at a whole new world,
hitting down with a big crash, just like a rock band!
I went back into the ship,
then I banged my hip and lip!
Going down all the way floating,
I'd rather I went boating!
Getting tickles in my tummy, dreaming of my pet bunny!
Still going to get my gravity back,
I hope, I hope I don't have jet lag.
Hitting the ground, most of them frowned,
especially looking around.
Parachute flying out, everyone looking about.
When I appeared, everyone had a good shout.
Hip, hip hooray! I'm back on Earth today!

Lucy Jackson (9)
St Angela's Primary School, Glasgow

My Space Poem

Space, space, such a wonderful place
I'd like to go there sometime,
I'd like to float around, not touch the ground
and meet some alien friends.

Aliens, aliens, will be my friends soon and
we'll play on the moon till afternoon.

The astronauts landed on the moon,
with a huge *kaboom.*
They say now we've landed on the moon
let's explore the world of the moon.

Lindsey Boyle (9)
St Angela's Primary School, Glasgow

MY SPACE POEM

I'm going to *space*
What a wonderful place
I'll take some make-up, just in case
I want to put in on my face
While I float all around the place.

I landed on the *moon*
With a big, massive *boom*
It's a shame I have to go soon
Because it's nearly noon

Then suddenly this strange creature
Asked what I was,
And I said I was a teacher

I quickly wrote a note
And put it in a toy boat
I flung it down to Earth
And hoped it would land in my town, Perth

I walked into my *spaceship*
And counted 10, 9, 8, 7, 6, 5, 4, 3, 2, 1
Blast-off, I was on my way down to Earth
To land in my own town, Perth.

Kimberley Hendry (9)
St Angela's Primary School, Glasgow

WORLD WAR II

World War II started in 1939,
Before that everything was fine.
Soldiers as brave as a bear faced up to their fears.
World War II lasted for 6 long years,
Adolf Hitler was as cruel as Cruella De Vil.
No one dared to go near window sills
Because Germans waited and prepared for the kill.
As people are crushed in the air-raids and pray,
Wondering if the war will end on the 8th of May.
The bombs were like a door slamming,
The war ended in 1945
And everyone tried to lead ordinary lives.

Lyndsay MacSween (12)
St Angela's Primary School, Glasgow

WORLD WAR II

W orld War II was a terrible thing
O ver the world there was lots of suffering
R ulers fought
L eaders led
D ying soldiers . . . wounded . . . dead

W ar is evil, so they say
A nd yet we still fight today
R ound the world people cried

II many hurt, too many died.

Tariq Boussouara (10)
St Angela's Primary School, Glasgow

THE VOYAGE

Today at ten, we danced outside laughing happily
as time ran by. But over the hills a man came clear
wearing a hat which was torn. One glove, a bag
and a pair of boots, trousers, a shirt all covered
in soot.

To us he said, 'A story can I tell about a voyage over
sea,' he sat and said '200 years ago a
man named Dan made a plan to sail across the sea.
The boat it went on and on till at last the boat came
to a stop.'
'Ha ha,' said a voice near, not far.
'I'm a pirate,' he said and Dan jumped off, 'the coward'
and swam ten metres and
                      drowned,
                      drowned,
                      drowned.

Alas the man said, 'Now I go, remember the story of the voyage.'

Ryan Hooper (11)
St Angela's Primary School, Glasgow

DOLPHINS

D olphins are graceful creatures,
O h! How swiftly they glide.
L iving in and loving their emerald blue sea,
P laying all day long,
H aving so much fun.
I   do wish I could stay,
N ever having to go away.
S taying there forever. Yes! Let's stay there forever.

Rachael Docherty (11)
St Angela's Primary School, Glasgow

My Space Dream!

Once I had fascinating dream,
I went to space on a submarine,
I then landed on the moon,
with a great big, big boom!
I then got out and looked around,
I was floating far from the ground.
I was floating up and down . . .
and moving all around!
I finally fell down and went into my submarine,
flew away back to Earth
to continue my dream!

Aislinn Dowling (9)
St Angela's Primary School, Glasgow

Whale's Dance

W hales are
H uge
A nd
L ovely animals
E normous
S ilent as the moon.

D ancing
A nd
N ice
C olourful
E legant.

Erin Tierney (9)
St Bartholomew's Primary School, Glasgow

IN THE GARDEN

In the olive bush
Lay a little puppy
Falling asleep.

Flying about the air
There is a bee
Looking about for honey.

Up on the wall
Sits a white cat
Purring quietly.

Under the pile of leaves
A family of hedgehogs
Are asleep.

Up the acorn tree
Is a furry squirrel
Looking for acorns.

In the shed
There is a rabbit
It is scared of the fox.

Up on the birdhouse
Sits a robin
Eating the seeds.

Nicola Mulheron (9)
St Bartholomew's Primary School, Glasgow

COLOURS OF CHRISTMAS

Christmas is red.

Red is the colour of ice-chilled noses.
Red is the cherry on top of the pudding.
Red is the colour of the children's joy
When they are waiting for Santa Claus.
Red is the colour of Santa's sparkling suit.

Christmas is green.

Green is the colour of the sparkling presents
Under its evergreen branch.
Green is the colour of the banging crackers
Waiting to be split in a huge bang.
Green is the colour of the grass crouched
Down ready for spring.

Christmas is gold.

Gold is the shooting stars in the bright sky.
Gold is the colour of the crackers ready to crack.
The golden crust turkey is lying with a knife in
Its back ready to be eaten.

Josh Henderson (9)
St Bartholomew's Primary School, Glasgow

SPIDERS

S piders are creepy
P rowling around
I n and out of corners
D ark places and ground
E ating flies and making webs
R esting at night at the bottom of your bed.

Natalie Casci (9)
St Cadoc's Primary School, Glasgow

MY WORLD

My world, my world, my world is called Party World.
Don't mention school in my world cause school is extinct
in my world.
All there is, is parties, parties and more parties.
No one skips a party, disco or ball in my world.
If anyone skips a party in my land
they will be thrown out of Party World and into
the land of schools.
Party World's nickname is Planet Pop.
The most exciting thing about it is
boys don't exist in my world
nobody is grounded in my world.

Katrina Evans (8)
St Cadoc's Primary School, Glasgow

NUMBER POEM

Number one I ate a bun
Number two it was true
Number three it is all about me
Number four I fell through the floor
Number five I kicked a bee hive
Number six I ate Weetabix
Number seven I'll go to Heaven
Number eight I made a new mate
Number nine I feel fine
Number ten I saw a hen.

Patrick Hamill (8)
St Cadoc's Primary School, Glasgow

TIGGER

Tigger was a lovely kitten and I knew he'd always be.
I'll never forget now friendly he was and how he loved me.
We got him in October when the leaves began to fall.
He always would come running whenever I did call.

Tigger loved to chase things, he loved to climb up trees,
Especially the Christmas one and Mum she wasn't pleased.
He broke some of the branches, he knocked the baubles down,
But Mum said she wouldn't mind that if he were still around.

Tigger loved to sit on me and I would stroke his fur,
I knew that he was happy because he used to purr.
Our neighbours all knew Tigger, they thought he was good fun,
He really was a special cat loved by everyone.

It was a cold and frosty morning the day that Tigger died
And ever since that morning I've cried and cried and cried,
I'll always remember Tigger as he was my best friend,
And wherever you are now Tigger, to you my love I send.

Suzanne Oswald (8)
St Cadoc's Primary School, Glasgow

MY LITTLE SISTER

My little sister is a baby,
The naughtiest little baby you've ever seen.
She stood on the sink
And covered it in ink,
Then said, 'That was me!'

My little sister is a baby,
The cheekiest little baby you've ever seen.
She hit the cat
With a cricket bat,
Then said, 'That wasn't me!'

Siobhan Cameron (8)
St Cadoc's Primary School, Glasgow

A DOG CALLED MOLLY

My cousin Paula has a
new dog called Molly,
he is small, always
happy and very jolly.

She runs and jumps and
nips and bites,
and she likes to rip your
tights!

Her coat is black, soft
and shiny,
and she is very, very tiny!

She woofs and woofs all
through the night,
but she is precious,
special and a puppy I
would love to have
especially because she
is so bright!

Sarah Wallace (8)
St Cadoc's Primary School, Glasgow

MY TEDDY

My teddy's name is Ted
I cuddle him in bed
I've had him since I was small
and I'll love him till I'm very tall.

I rub my nose with his tail
it helps me sleep, it never fails.
I dream of things that we can do
me, my teddy and my family too.

His fur is fluffy pink and white
his ears are small, his eyes are bright.
He rattles when I hold him close
I love my teddy, everyone knows.

Amy Ford (8)
St Cadoc's Primary School, Glasgow

IF I HAD A WISH

I wish I could fly
All over the sky
I would land on the beach
Just out of Mum's reach.

I wish I had a dog
I would take him for a jog
Down to the park
Before it gets dark
Then home to be fed
Then straight into bed.

Jennifer Lynn (7)
St Cadoc's Primary School, Glasgow

My Terrible Brother

My brother likes to fight
And he makes a lot of noise.
He always thinks he's right
When he breaks up all my toys.

My brother likes to play in the mud,
He's sad when it's nice weather.
He splashes in the rain with a thud,
Then takes my neighbour's heather.

My brother's a wild animal,
He should be in a cage.
He really is a cannibal,
He bites me in a rage.

My brother's Mr Greedy Guts.
He has no time to play.
I'd say he's absolutely nuts.
He has everything his way.

Sean Pickering (9)
St Cadoc's Primary School, Glasgow

Christmas

Follow that star that shines so bright,
Follow that star all through the night.
So that you can see the child lying in a manger.
Then you will not feel like a complete stranger.

Amy Rowe (8)
St Cadoc's Primary School, Glasgow

MY PET

In the house in the middle of the night,
My pet will give you a huge big fright.
Creeping, turning, in you come.
A very scary mystery, a tiny wee crumb.
Follow that crumb into the house,
Oh my goodness it's a tiny wee mouse!

He's got big pink eyes and fur so smooth,
A big long tail that waggles when he moves.
He starts running slow then gets faster and faster
And stops to think - then bursts out with laughter!
When the time comes to say goodbye
He scuttles away and I have a sigh.

Fiona Pittman (8)
St Cadoc's Primary School, Glasgow

WHEN I GROW UP

When I grow up
I want to be
An accountant
I love to save money
It gives me a tickle
In my tummy
Don't laugh
It's not funny
Serious business
Counting money.

Emma Anderson (9)
St Cadoc's Primary School, Glasgow

A Day In The Country

I went for a walk in the country
Wearing my summer hat,
I climbed a fence into a field
And fell in a big cow pat!

I stood up to clean my lovely dress,
I didn't know where to turn,
I took a few steps backwards and fell into a burn!

I crawled out of the water,
I really felt a fool,
I climbed the fence into the field
To be chased by a big black bull!

Joanne McKenna (10)
St Hilary's Primary School, Glasgow

When The Chip Went Swimming

A chip went swimming
One day in May
He did not realise he had to pay
He went into his pocket and pulled out his locket

The chip could not find any money
Everyone thought it was funny
Then the chip felt something in his tummy
He went crying to his mummy
The poor little chip.

Katie Thomson (10)
St Hilary's Primary School, Glasgow

I FEEL SOMETHING . . .

I feel something tingling in my toes,
I think it's a creature with a very big nose,
It's been in my toes for a very long time
And I think he's a miner because he's managed to make
A very large hole on my big toe.

My mum took me to the doctor but he's a bad talker
So I couldn't hear what to do,
Then she took me to hospital:
They said, 'You've got a problem and you need some medicine.'

I took some medicine and it made my skin grown
And the creature has disappeared too,
But there's a spot there instead now!

Elaine Veitch (10)
St Hilary's Primary School, Glasgow

ON MY BIRTHDAY

On my birthday when I wake up
I shout hooray because it's a special day.
I get lots of presents too
And people pop out and say 'Boo.'

On my birthday I get the bumps
And after that I get big lumps of cake.
Then I take a last look at this day and go to bed,
Then the next morning I feel thumps in my head.

Emma Fulton (10)
St Hilary's Primary School, Glasgow

CREEPY FREAKY!

A ghost lives in my house
Last night it ate my mouse
It's creepy and it's freaky

A ghost lives in my house
I found its tail in the mail
It's creepy and it's freaky

A ghost lives in my house
When I found its tail
I kind of went pale,
Do you know what?
It's creepy and it's freaky.

Michael Cusack (10)
St Hilary's Primary School, Glasgow

THERE'S SOMETHING IN MY BED

There's something in my bed,
I feel it at my head,
I know it's under my pillow,
Oh dear, it's just Mr Willow.

It is my cuddly toy,
That I play with quite a lot,
Oh, that little toy,
I think I've lost the plot!

Katy Gallagher (10)
St Hilary's Primary School, Glasgow

I Am An Alien (Or Not . . .)

I am an alien,
here's proof if you don't believe me.

One day far, far away,
Aliens came to play!
I ran down and said,
'I'm not an alien!'
Doh! I thought obviously
'Cut, cut, cut'
Moaned the cameraman.
So the thing is
I'm *not an alien!*
And guess what,
I was fired!
Boo! Hoo!

Gordon Quinn (10)
St Hilary's Primary School, Glasgow

Hallowe'en

When I go out at Hallowe'en
Many a monster can be seen,
Vampires, warlocks, bats and cats
And even witches in pointy hats.
So when you go out and about that night,
Don't be surprised when you get a
Fright!

Daniel Law (10)
St Hilary's Primary School, Glasgow

The Singer Of This Song

The singer of this song
is as loud as a parrot
she squeaks, squawks and can't sing for long
she's as mad as a carrot

As hard as a rock
as thin as a rake
as sharp as a tack
as sleek as a snake

As sly as a fox
as happy as a sandboy
as strong as an ox
as free as a bird

The singer of this song
is as mad as a hatter
the singer writes
one singer one song.

Julie Marie Blake (11)
St Hilary's Primary School, Glasgow

The Ghost

The other night I went down the stair,
Only to find someone sitting there!
I ran up to my room and locked the door with a broom.
I hid behind the door as scared as a cat,
In one hand a golf club and the other a bat.
I heard whaling and screaming, no one around,
It's just me alone!

David McGeever (10)
St Hilary's Primary School, Glasgow

OUR TERRIBLE TOILET

My toilet has done a terrible thing,
It swallowed up my sister's ring.
She was annoyed with what I'd done,
So I built up a very fast run.

I ran and ran until I stopped and
On my neck my head just popped!
It was a very terrible thing,
All because of my sister's ring!

The funeral was so, so bad,
Most of my family were really sad,
I went up to heaven and God just said,
'Oh my god, where's your head?'

Michael Linskey (10)
St Hilary's Primary School, Glasgow

MY SCHOOL

It's not my place to run the train
The whistle I can't blow
It's not my place to say how far
The train's allowed to go
It's not my place to shoot off steam
Nor even dang the bell
But let the whole thing
Jump the track
And see who comes out well.

James Fowlie (11)
St Hilary's Primary School, Glasgow

TEACHERS

If we are sad,
The teacher will not say we are bad.
If you do not do your work,
The teacher will shout
And you will get a clout on the ear.

If the teacher said, 'Do not talk,'
You should not.
On the board the teacher will write with chalk,
The teacher said 'Draw a pot for art.'

So teachers are really *not* that fun!

Gemma Connolly (10)
St Hilary's Primary School, Glasgow

3

My poem has 3 lines
And 3 words in each line
I read the poem at 5 to 3
I finished the poem at 3 o'clock
I'm only joking, I'm only 3
I don't know how to read remember
I'm only 3
I have 3 more years before I read
I only know 3 words
They are 3, 3 and 3.

Kevin O'Boyle (10)
St Hilary's Primary School, Glasgow

MY BEST FRIEND

My best friend is orange.
She's a sunny summer's day
in a hot sauna.
She is a hot summer sun in the sky.
She is a mini-skirt
and a messy couch.
She is Neighbours
and a hot plate of potatoes.

Mhairi Stringer (11)
St Hilary's Primary School, Glasgow

MY FRIEND, MEGAN

Megan is yellow.
She is a bright summer day
in the park.
She can sometimes be a rainy day
but she is a nice T-shirt.
Megan is a tall chair
and is as funny as Friends,
but most of all she is sweets.

Caroline Anne McHugh (11)
St Hilary's Primary School, Glasgow

BECUS I CUD NOT SPEL

Becus I cud not spel that wel
Everybudy laffed
My teecher, Mum, Dad and dug
And eeven half my class!

It's not becus I'm daft
I just don't no how to spel
My bruver said it's normall
But I don't no how to spel!

Katie Baptie (10)
St Hilary's Primary School, Glasgow

FOOTBALL

Football is green.
It's a warm summer's morning
in a huge stadium.
It's a burning day
in a football strip.
It's an expensive waterbed.
It's the Scottish league
and a bag of chips.

James Scanlan (10)
St Hilary's Primary School, Glasgow

TJ

TJ is green.
He is a spring morning
in a jungle gym.
He is a snowy day.
He is a cap turned backwards
and an untidy desk.
He is recess
and an ordered pizza and cola.

Richard Lynn (11)
St Hilary's Primary School, Glasgow

I'VE ALWAYS WONDERED

I've always wondered about the planets
Why there are nine and not just one?
I've always wondered about the stars
Why there are millions and not just five?
But the one thing I've always wondered about is
What is the universe? What can it be?
And why is it so very far from me?

Emma Fletcher (11)
St Hilary's Primary School, Glasgow

SCOTLAND

Scotland is happy.
Scotland is not sad.
Scotland is the place
that makes me glad.
The weather is bad.
The atmosphere is not sad.
Scotland is for me and you.

Stephen Dickson (11)
St Hilary's Primary School, Glasgow

ALIENS

Aliens are weird and pointy.
They ride about in silly saucepans.
They talk so fast and funny,
It makes you want to scream.
If we ever meet them,
We will faint and think it was a dream.

Christopher John Barbara (11)
St Hilary's Primary School, Glasgow

THE REF RAP

Clap clap
Clap clap clap
Clap clap clap clap
Clap clap

I don't win
I don't lose
I point the finger
Uphold the rules

I show the card
I send them off
I blow the whistle
When I've had enough

Clap clap
Clap clap clap
Clap clap clap clap
Clap clap.

Daniel McAinsh (11)
St Hilary's Primary School, Glasgow

FOOTBALL

Football is multicoloured.
It is a warm summer day
in a giant stadium.
It is a blazing hot sunny day.
It is a dirty T-shirt
and a big bench.
It is Match of the Day.
It is a hot pie.

Stephen Dingwall (11)
St Hilary's Primary School, Glasgow

FOOTBALL

We all love football,
Oh yes we do,
Adults and children even grandparents too.
There's Celtic and Rangers
Plus Man U,
For we all love football,
Oh yes we do.
There's Petta and Larsson
And Mols too,
For we all love football,
Even you!
We all like *Celtic*,
Oh yes we do,
We even like *Rangers*.
For they're quite good too.
For we all *love football*,
Oh yes we do!

Claire Neil (11)
St Hilary's Primary School, Glasgow

MY FRIEND

Carrie is orange.
She is a warm summer's day.
She is the hot sandy beach.
She is the sunshine on a cloudy day.
She is a pair of leather trousers.
She is a leopard-skin rug.
She is Popstars
and a slice of pizza.

Stefanie Kennedy (11)
St Hilary's Primary School, Glasgow

HAPPINESS

Happiness is when Manchester United won the Treble.
Happiness is when it's Christmas morning.
Happiness is when Kane and the Undertaker win the tag team titles.
Happiness is when I got a new puppy.
Happiness is when we go out for a nice meal.
Happiness is when the whole family gets together.
Happiness is when I go to stay over at my friends.
Happiness is when I score a goal.
Happiness is when you win a competition.
Happiness is when we go on our trip to Ardentinny.

Greg Lemon (11)
St Hilary's Primary School, Glasgow

HAPPINESS

Happiness is the start of summer holidays.
Happiness is when you win the lottery.
Happiness is your birthday.
Happiness is when you go to Disneyland.
Happiness is when you finish your homework.
Happiness is playing football.
Happiness is when my brother visits.
Happiness is when your mum and dad pay £12 to watch something on Sky Box Office.

Daniel Guy (11)
St Hilary's Primary School, Glasgow

MY MUM

My mum is a burnt orange.
She is a sweltering hot day
in sunny Italy.
She is a shining star.
She is a black top,
a lava lamp
and a hot, delicious,
creamy cappuccino.

Christina Lila Midgley (11)
St Hilary's Primary School, Glasgow

DEATH CAMP

Dead bodies piled on top of each
other like wood on a fire.

Burnt flesh as the bodies are
taken away.

My ribs which are sticking through
my stretched skin.

The blood in my mouth from this
morning's beating.

Children screaming as they are taken
away from their parents.

The sadness and sorrow as children
are beaten up; . . .

Concentration camp.

Ashleigh Buchan (11)
St Jerome's Primary School, Glasgow

BERGEN BELSEN

B attered and flogged are innocent people,
E ngaged with fear, death is all they think of,
R ummaging bins for scraps of food,
G oing home is a distant thought,
E liminating Jews one by one,
N owhere to go, nowhere to run.

B utchering them like farm animals,
E very tear is a drink of water,
L ugubrious Jewish children scream for their parents,
S adistic Germans murder and slaughter,
E very drop of blood is a game to them,
N o one should die like that ever again.

Sean McGhee (12)
St Jerome's Primary School, Glasgow

BERGEN BELSEN

B rutal beatings every day,
E ndless hunger, sickness and bleeding,
R acist remarks are all we hear,
G ory are the facts of the camp,
E scape is impossible from this terrible place,
N owhere to go, no one to turn to.

B loody dead bodies litter the floor,
E vil we see as we walk through the door,
L iving on crumbs of bread that make my stomach sore,
S inister people try and break our bones,
E verlasting injuries, worry and hope,
N ever could you imagine the things I'm going through.

Peter McGowan (11)
St Jerome's Primary School, Glasgow

BERGEN BELSEN

B eaten up every day by the Nazi soldiers,
E very day innocent people are shot in the head,
R ed is the colour of blood flowing from the hole in my head,
G uns going off in the middle of the night,
E ven children have been told to do hard work,
N ot even adults have their freedom.

B abies crying as they're taken away from their parents,
E veryone dying because they have typhus,
L ittle children die of hunger,
S oldiers coming to rescue us,
E ven though only a few people lived,
N azi soldiers killing everybody they see.

Kevin Callaghan (11)
St Jerome's Primary School, Glasgow

NIGHTMARE AT AUSCHWITZ

A disease killing my friends and terrorising
the camp,
The disease and fear of small children.
The dead carcasses being burned in a hot
fiery furnace,
My bones that go through my elastic skin.
The agonising cries of dying children.
A sickening sickness tearing me apart,
piece by piece . . .
Nightmare at Auschwitz . . .!

Daryl Knox (11)
St Jerome's Primary School, Glasgow

BERGEN BELSEN

B lood on my head from being hit by a gun,
E ating mouldy bread with maggots crawling all over,
R acism of Jews is endless,
G assing innocent people for their colour or religion,
E ndless pain and torture,
N ever being free again.

B eing bullied every day for nothing,
E ver dreaming of peace all around the world,
L ove from nobody ever again?
S hattered memories of the past,
E vil all around you,
N othing to live for anymore.

Colette Mackenzie (11)
St Jerome's Primary School, Glasgow

NIGHTMARES

A lways watching people dying,
U sed to the smell of burning bodies,
S inging to keep our hopes up,
C hallenging tasks after we are beaten,
H ow could people be this cruel?
W aiting for our hour to die,
I watch my family being killed,
T omorrow might not come,
Z ombies are what we are like.

Sean Ferguson (11)
St Jerome's Primary School, Glasgow

BERGEN BELSEN

B lood on the walls from everyone's beating,
E veryone screaming and screeching,
R acism towards other people,
G assing and people being killed,
E veryone thinking their families are dead,
N ame calling and fighting.

B ones sticking out like daggers and swords,
E ndless beatings and deaths all around
L oneliness and pain is endless
S platters of blood all over my face,
E veryone being put in gas chambers,
N azis shooting and killing people.

Kim Marie Bradley (11)
St Jerome's Primary School, Glasgow

MY LIVING HELL

B odies lying everywhere I look,
E verything I try to touch I cannot feel,
R acism is sweeping the camp,
G uts splattered all over my face,
E veryone is trying to survive but there is no chance of life,
N o one is going to live - well that's what I think.

B attering me as I try to get away,
E ver lasting horror as they kill someone else,
L ifting the gun and I think they are going to shoot me,
S mashing me over the face with a cup,
E nter the death list - I think I'm going to be next,
N o please, don't shoot, nooo . . . Boom!

Jonathan Ralston (11)
St Jerome's Primary School, Glasgow

ACID RAIN

Fat pipes out of a factory, pouring out smoke like
Chugging old steam trains.

Fluffy clouds, mixing with old smoke like cake mix
Being mixed with an electric whisk.

Rain falling from the deep blue sky,
Like a gushing waterfall.

Deadly acid rain, stabbing and killing
Beautiful green grass plants.

Plants and animals left dead
Like ice cream white skeletons.

Kieran Devlin (10)
St Louise's Primary School, Glasgow

OIL SPILLS

O tters dying, seagulls flying,
I 'll try to stop the oil spill,
L ittle fish, fishermen trying to kill.

S pilling oil,
P ollution and you are trying to spoil,
I n the sea, in the soil,
L ittle insects are going to die,
L ow in the soil the fish have gone, bye-bye,
S o don't try to make our fish die.

Greg Galbraith (11)
St Louise's Primary School, Glasgow

FRIGHT NIGHT

I'm lying stiff, I've heard a noise
That's out of the ordinary
I shut my eyes tight, it's 01:00am
I'm meant to be asleep
Oh no, the door is opening
Who is coming in?
'This is fright night' say the demons
Now here comes the headless man
He is really scary
'It's fright night' say the goblins
Opening my eyes I feel a shiver running
Down my spine
What is happening? They're coming up the
Ladder to my bed
I scream again and again, they're beside me now
Shaking me, aaaarrrggghh!
'Oh Mum, it's only you, I thought you were a ghost'
'Ha' Mum said and walked out the room.
'See you next fright night' she muttered.
Oh no!

Stacey Anne Quinn (10)
St Louise's Primary School, Glasgow

A FLYING BIKE

A fiery blast
A suffocating cover
Flying very fast
Constant ear pains
Batteries always running out
My flying bike machine.

Kieran Rooney (10)
St Louise's Primary School, Glasgow

In The Lion's Cage

I am lying beside a high and beautiful golden haystack.
I see prowling claws; I also see a mouth swaying.
I hear paws dancing and I hear a tail prancing along.
I smell the sweetness of the air.
I taste the smell of his last meal, I taste the exotic spices.
I feel his warm breath on me, I feel him coming nearer to me.

Nicola Claffey (10)
St Louise's Primary School, Glasgow

Happy

My happy colour is shimmering gold.
It tastes like my favourite dessert, chocolate cake.
It smells like my favourite meal, pizza.
It looks like the bright sun shining brightly above me.
It sounds like the birds singing to me in the springtime.
It feels like my mum hugging me.

Lisa McCarron (11)
St Louise's Primary School, Glasgow

The Lion

I am lying beside a golden wall
I see paws charging
I hear grinding paws itching to pounce
I smell beer from the hot breath
I taste hair flying in the air
I touch lumpy custard
I feel agitated, nervy, I'm trapped in its den.

Nicole Bradley (10)
St Louise's Primary School, Glasgow

ENVIRONMENT

E very day humans destroy a piece of Earth,
N o more of this must happen,
V ery soon we will destroy all,
I f this goes on our Earth and animals will die out,
R ivers are being polluted, fish are dying,
O ur Earth is dying,
N obody is doing anything about it,
M any animals are extinct already,
E verything is in danger,
N othing is being done,
T his Earth is dying.

Samantha Weldon (11)
St Louise's Primary School, Glasgow

MY MUM

She is a red onion.
She is a nutty topic.
She is a big cookery book.
She is a healthy and crunchy vitamin.
She is a Whitney Houston song.
She is a white overall.
She is shimmering make-up.
She is shiny pink medicine.
She is dark brown bottles.
She is a little brown tablet.
She is a lovely toiletries set.

Lyndsay Swan (11)
St Louise's Primary School, Glasgow

THE POETRY HOUSE

Come and I will show you my house as we walk along this zigzag path made from red, blue, yellow and pink pencils.

Do you like my letterbox, it is a lion's mouth, pull his tongue and look you have entered my house.

My lovely floor as you can see is made of gold. Did you know it's 24 carat gold?

As we move in now to the living room you can see the jungle in the fireplace.

Can you hear all the different sounds like the tigers roaring, elephants squealing and birds chirping?

Look at my staircase made from sparkling jewels, come on everyone, stand on the red ruby and it will take you up to the top.

What's that door at the end of the corridor with a gold star for a handle?
Open it and look at the toilet seat, its a shark's mouth.

Look at the sink, it's shaped as a rubber with a key for a tap.

Next to the bathroom is my room, open the book. Done it? Then write the code which is 17789 then close it and voila you have now entered my room. Now when you are in my room you have to be careful.

No, no, no, don't touch!
My crystal ball will turn you into a ghost. Oh, too late!

Cheryl Louise Hume (11)
St Louise's Primary School, Glasgow

TIGER

T iger, tiger, your fur so sleek,
I n the darkness, just take a peek
   at the man right over there,
   he's evil, now that's just not fair!
G rowl, tiger growl, he's foul, tiger foul!
E vil men are after you, is it true that you feel blue?
R un, tiger run, or your life will soon be done!

Laura McGarrell (11)
St Louise's Primary School, Glasgow

A HILL VIEW

A blue sky shaped like a pie
Big hills like polar bears
Curly bushes like my gran's hair
Big houses slim and fat
Dark shadows, jumbo and tiny
Wooden gates, big and small
White snow, that could glow.

Michael Quigley (8)
St Machan's Primary School, Glasgow

FROM OUR CLASSROOM WINDOW

Huge hills, big and cold, towering over us.
Graceful trees, soft and swish, dancing around.
Awkward rocks, sharp and hidden on the hills,
Pokey grass, brown and dewy and all frosty.

Brick houses, dirty or clean, with slate roofs.
Broken fences, wiry and splintery, tall and small.
House shadows, dark and gloomy, making shade.
Rusty gates, bashed and dirty, cutting Dad.

Roisin Convery (9)
St Machan's Primary School, Glasgow

FROM OUR CLASSROOM WINDOW

The big, tall hills, rough and steep,
The clear sky so innocent and free,
Jaggy gates so strong and fierce,
Fluffy snow, so white and cold.

Huge trees, bold and bare,
The bush on the hills so rusty and noisy,
Rows of houses taller than me,
Dark shadows grey and dull.

Daryl Robertson (9)
St Machan's Primary School, Glasgow

FROM OUR CLASSROOM WINDOW

Clear sky, clear and free,
Covered hills with soft fluff,
Bare trees looking for the leaves,
Houses at the top looking down on me.

Covered rocks filled with snow,
Reddish grass trying to grow,
Bushes have got shadows,
Brownish hills looking down at the ground.

Kirsten Hardie (9)
St Machan's Primary School, Glasgow

My Friends

Nicola is far older than me!
Melissa is as cute as can be!
Anna is the youngest of three!
It's good to have friends.

To me Seana isn't well known!
Her big brother Josh is nearly full-grown!
Robert doesn't like to be alone!
I like to have friends.

Then there's me!
Perfect little me!
Eldest of three,
I'm my best friend!

Claire Neilan (10)
St Peter's Primary School, Glasgow

Music

Playing the piano is lots of fun,
It has a tune for everyone.
Playing 'Forte' is quite loud,
While 'Pianissimo' calms the crowd.
'Staccato' makes the notes all dance,
'Legato' puts them in a trance.
'Rallentando' calms down their fire,
'Accelerando' inspires the choir.
'Adagio's' the way tortoises walk,
'Allegro's' the way that chatterboxes talk.

Stephanie Man (11)
St Peter's Primary School, Glasgow

THE PHOENIX

The phoenix is,
as graceful as a station,
the flames on its body will burn as long as time,
as hot as molten lava,
it bends its firey head down
into a stream of lava,
as hot as a dragon's flame,
and drinks its fill.

But behold! The phoenix turns gold!
It spreads its firey wings,
each one as long as a metre
and flies towards the sun.

But alas! It has begun!
The phoenix shall rule this earth,
as greatly as a king.

Laura McSheffrey (10)
St Peter's Primary School, Glasgow

TIGERS

Tigers are as cute as can be,
but as fierce as a dinosaur roaming the city.
They are as furry as a squirrel's tail,
as wild as a child when the weather is mild.
They're as playful as a puppy and would
definitely eat a ducky.
So if you want to see one, go to the zoo
and you will see one too!

Sinead McLaughlin (10)
St Peter's Primary School, Glasgow

COMPUTER GAMES

Nintendo 64 is cool,
Sometimes it can make me drool.
The best game is Donkey Kong,
It's because he is so strong.
Multiplayers are so great,
You can play it with yer mate.

PlayStation is so fab,
I love reading their cool mag.
Their best game has got to be,
Final Fantasy number three.

The Sega Mega Drive is not new,
Their best game is Shinobi Two.
The second best is owned by me,
And it is known as Sonic Three.

But the PC is the best,
Better than all the rest.
Their best game is without a doubt,
Majesty, let's give it a shout,
Computers!

Anthony Cosimini (10)
St Peter's Primary School, Glasgow

TASMANIAN TIGERS

Tigers are;
as wide-mouthed as a T-rex,
as sleek as can be,
as fast as a cheetah,
as deadly as a velociraptor,
tigers are cool.

Mark Tully (10)
St Peter's Primary School, Glasgow

SCHOOL

Every night I dread the next day
because at school they bully me.
Every day when I play games
they come up to me and call me names.
If I tell the teacher on them,
they'll make up lies and say I'm kiddin'.

David Smith (10)
St Peter's Primary School, Glasgow

MONKEYS

As agile as a swing door.
As cute as can be.
As hairy as a long-haired dog.
As boisterous as a little boy in his terrible twos.
Monkeys, monkeys, they are cute.

Nicolle Campbell (10)
St Peter's Primary School, Glasgow

SUMMER

Summer is a happy time,
The scent of flowers is divine,
The sun is warm upon my face
And winter's gone to another place,
Yes! I love summertime.

David Whitehill (11)
St Peter's Primary School, Glasgow

POPPIES

I see a sea of red, red poppies
All bending in the breeze,
All brilliant in the morning light
For everyone to see.
A river of red that stretches for miles
And goes on from field to field,
Gives calmness and peace,
In a war that should cease
To a heart that needs to be healed.

In the evening I light a candle
And remember my long lost love,
Who gave his life so long ago
And is waiting for me above.
The poppies grow and mark the place
Where my true love lies at peace,
He gave his life so we could live
And the evils of war would cease.

Rachel Johnstone (11)
St Peter's Primary School, Glasgow

THE BULLY

The bully picks on younger boys,
He takes their money and their toys.
I asked the teacher what to do -
She didn't even have a clue.
So I had to plead on bended knee,
But she just sat and drank her tea.

Ross Boyle (11)
St Peter's Primary School, Glasgow

PLAYTIME AT SCHOOL

When it's playtime in my school,
All my friends say,
'What a waste!'
They shout all day saying,
'Boo! Boo!'
I mean it's like being in World War II.
They know it is always bad,
But they hate the way the teachers call them 'Lad!'
They like school,
They just don't know it.
They might hate it,
Just a bit.
Well, I like school, that's all I know.
So does my friend
We call him 'Big Moe'.

Kashif Din (10)
St Peter's Primary School, Glasgow

ALLIGATORS

Alligators have got teeth
as sharp as blades.
Backs as lumpy as porridge.
Skin as tough as old leather
and eyes black with evil.
Ready always to pounce
upon its prey.

Sam Tulleth (9)
St Peter's Primary School, Glasgow

RATS

Rats are,
As wriggly as a worm.
As sharp as a razor.
As sneaky and fierce as a fox.
Rats, rats, wonderful rats.

Kerri Whitelaw (10)
St Peter's Primary School, Glasgow

CLEAR AND SIMPLE

On a subject of my choice,
In a clear and simple voice,
In my school and in my house,
Through my mind and books I browse.
It is late and I am tired -
Still I try to be inspired,
But it's hard to think of words
Good enough to charm the birds.
Now it's dawn, the sun is up,
Still I find I am stuck.
So to bed instead I go,
Without a single line to show.

Rachael Aitken (11)
Tinto Primary School

THE AIR RAID

The siren went I was
in my bed. My ears
were ringing and tingling.
I was crying, I was tired.
My mum came in and
we ran down the stairs.
It was dark, pitch-black.
I couldn't see a thing.
We went along the muddy
grass to the Anderson shelter,
'Safe at last' I cried.
I hope.

Danielle Sharkey (11)
West Coats Primary School

WAR TIME

Evacuation when
children are taken from home.
Violent bombers and
soldiers marching and
flying around.
Ahhhh, the sound of a
siren shrieking in my ear.
'Where have all the
children gone?' someone shouts.
At last the war has ended.

Alice Watson (11)
West Coats Primary School

I Can't Sleep

I can't sleep for all the horrendous
noises. I stay awake with the siren still
going and all the thousands of people
screaming. The bombs screeching down
and that one was for me!

Deborah Wilson (11)
West Coats Primary School

This Is War

The siren rings.
We hear the radio saying that we are at war
with Germany.
We get scared.
We start to scream.
We are all going to die.
My world has totally changed.

Joanne Lang (11)
West Coats Primary School

War

Off went the convoy of Hurricanes,
I wish Hitler were sane,
It's like one big firework,
As the Hurricane flies by,
Down swoops a Stuka,
Off goes our bazooka,
Bang.

Jamie McPherson (11)
West Coats Primary School

WAR

The Germans started to take over
In 1939.
If we didn't put up blackout curtains,
We would pay a fine.
Winston Churchill was the best,
He would never, ever rest,
'Til Hitler got what he deserved,
(Some people thought he had a nerve.)
British officers they fought
And they never, ever forgot,
That this was the middle of World War II,
So they fought 'til their faces were red and not blue
And our tears went away,
On that special D-Day.

Alison Louise Wright (11)
West Coats Primary School

ALL ALONE

I was standing in the playground,
In a corner all alone.
I felt so sad,
Everyone else was glad.
Why couldn't it be me,
Shouting out with glee,
Or playing happily with children
Around the trees?
I felt so sad,
Everyone else was glad,
Why couldn't it be me?

Louise Thomson (11)
West Coats Primary School

A DRIZZLE OF BOMBS

A drizzle of bombs fell from the sky.
The sky black,
Houses alight.
A terrible sight to see!
Across the road Mrs Brown's house was hit!
No one hurt,
But that could have been me!
The velvet black sky roaring!
Planes dropping bombs left, right and centre.
A drizzle of bombs fell from the sky.
They caused great devastation.

Lori Allen (11)
West Coats Primary School

THE SHIELD OF SCOTLAND

Everyone wondering what is happening
They say a shield is coming with a battle
Well if you say it'll come today
I don't believe what you say
Why not I say because my cousin is coming to stay
The man is an English man
And he'll kill me if a saw this yin.
Here it is the shield of Scotland
Here's my cousin coming in an English top.
Let's get him them men
If he dies he'll come alive
And eat you all and that's not all
The England top is part of me
Let's not wait and see.

Kevin Grant (10)
Westfield Primary School

I Saw A Ghost

I saw a ghost
I ran away
Dare I go back to see him next day?
But I did - I don't know - why I don't know how
I said 'Hi!
My name's Tim'
He gave me a smiling grin.
I went there once, I went there twice,
I got old, I died in bed,
The angel came down to pat my head.
We fly about, we make good friends
And that is where my story ends.

Carrie McFadyen (9)
Westfield Primary School

The Monster

The monster is green
ugly and spotty
comes to your house
for some coffee.
Likes eating worms,
likes eating bugs,
likes having humans
for his lunch.
He has everything
in the world
everybody likes him
and he's the
coolest monster ever.

Emma Kirkland (10)
Westfield Primary School

THE VERY FAT MOUSE

There was a big house,
Which had a very fat mouse,
He ate a lot,
He's bigger than a pot,
He can't get out of the house,
One day he was needing
A very big feeding,
And almost squashed a small mouse.
So one day all the mice
Agreed it would be nice,
To get rid of that beast
After the feast,
And that is what they did.
They kicked him out,
Away from the house,
And found a new one in the bin.
Then all the mice thought
That the new mouse was bigger than a pot.
So the mice agreed
They would need
To find out who the mouse really was.
Then they found out
That the new mouse
Was the one
Who just wanted
To be friends again.

Duncan Howie (10)
Westfield Primary School

THE HORSE IN THE FIELD

The horse in the field
made a big squeal
ran from the field
from one to another
then he thought *I'll rest here*
then he felt my field is near.

His owner was shouting
and the horse was doubting
the weather was bad
when the owner became sad
the horse fell down and
made a frown.

He found a pen
went to his den
wrote a letter
to Mr Better
went to the stable
beside the table.

The horse decided
to go to the field
his owner found him
said 'Kick him out
we don't want you
you big fat doubt.'

Clair Wilson (10)
Westfield Primary School

THE LITTLE WHITE MOUSE

The sun filtered into the house,
Then I saw a little white mouse,
My dad was scared,
Jumped on the chair,
Then he lost his underwear.

I thought it was sad,
When my mum was mad,
Then I had a strange idea,
I told myself not to fear,
I made a jelly,
Then watched the telly.

I fed it to the mouse,
Then it ran right out the house,
My mum said I was bad
And sent me to my bed,
So that was the end
Of my little white friend.

Diane Baker (10)
Westfield Primary School

THE LONELY RABBIT

The lonely rabbit
wanted a carrot
and everyone said
no.

Do you want a carrot
you lonely rabbit
yes please
kind sir.

The lonely rabbit
hopped and leaped around
the garden.
The lonely rabbit
was not a lonely
rabbit because he
had a carrot . . .

Stephanie Milliken (10)
Westfield Primary School

THE GALAXY AND ALIENS

In the galaxy are millions of stars.
If you do something wrong you
don't get locked up in bars.
The sun is very bright,
it is like a big space light.
Some planets are very cold,
some planets are very old.
There is no gravity in space,
when you think about it,
it's really a cool place.
On another planet there might be life,
they might be the size of a dice.
They might know sums,
they even might eat plums.
They might be green, they might be blue,
but I'm telling you that I never knew.
They might attack us one day,
but if they do, we'll make them pay.

Lewis Johnstone (10)
Westfield Primary School

MY RABBIT

My rabbit
has big ears
it's like a hairy brown wig
chewing on a thin old twig
he plays in the sun all day
has a hutch with millions of hay
makes up his own games
by the way
his nickname is James
plays on the green
does not like to be seen
and cabbage! He's ever so mean
does not like carrots
they are orange
but fruit what a hoot
then one day
he was round the back and
taken by a cat
I was so unhappy
I feel better now
I have a dog
with brown and black fur
it's a he not a her.

Elissa Moffat (10)
Westfield Primary School

THE DRAGON

A dragon is tough
Green and scaly
Breathing out fire and smoke
Brave warriors and knights
Tried to fight
But were thrown away
Burnt, stamped on
The king tried, the dragon won
The king tried again
The dragon still won
The dragon was unstoppable
No sword worked
In went the knights
Out came the bones
Broken bodies and squashed knights
That is what the dragon has done.

Alan Bickerton (10)
Westfield Primary School

LYN ON THE SHORE

Tam swam through the sea so calm,
When he got tae the shore,
He could swim no more.

While lyn on the sand,
Wa the sun shining down on his hand
A bonnie lass stood like an angel in the air.

Her face so truly, heavenly fair,
Her nature grace, so void of art,
But I adore my sweetheart.

Yvonne Carchrie (11)
Whitelees Primary School

THE WEE BONNIE LASSIE

The wee bonnie lassie sat by the shore,
And a glass of squash she would pour.
The waves would roar, the wind would blow,
And little did she know,
The tide would come in, but no fear did she know!

No attention to donkeys trotting by,
If someone upset her no tear did she cry.
A glass of squash she would pour.
This is the wee bonnie lassie that sat by the shore.

No one knows why she sits by the shore,
Maybe it's her long lost father that she loves more.
Watching the tide come in and the tide go out
And listening to her father's spirit shout,
I will be with you soon in time
And soon again things will be fine.

Robyn Wade (11)
Whitelees Primary School

BILL AND LILL

Down the steep, steep hill
Lived a man called Bill,
With his sister called Lill
He was ten-foot tall,
With a sign on his wall saying
'Please do not disturb.'

Lill was her name, she was a real pain,
Every night when she tried to sleep,
She shouted 'Bill will you get me to sleep?'

One morning when they woke, Lill spoke,
She said, 'I've hurt my foot,'
So Bill had a look, and then took a book,
And said, 'Lill you have broken your foot!'

Emma Davie (11)
Whitelees Primary School

FROM BABY TO ADULT

When I was born I cried very loud
Even though my parents were proud
They were with me day and night
Making sure everything was alright.

I went from baby to an infant
Not overnight or in an instant
Through these years I learned to talk
Then trouble started, yes I could walk!

Then I was five and came to my school years
And then I had to face all my fears
The teacher taught me many things
For when I grew up to spread my wings.

Many years I spent at school
Having followed many a rule
Then time came I had to leave
My schooldays behind me I was pleased.

From teenager to adult went really fast
Some years were sad, others a blast
I'm grown up now so what the heck
I do not need to get things checked.

Now I'm an adult, fully grown
Married with children all of my own
I only hope that I can be
As good as the parents that stood by me.

David Bain (11)
Whitelees Primary School